Advance Pr
SMAR
For Bu:

"Practicing the Emotional Intelligence techniques in *SMART EMOTIONS* is like having a trusted friend by your side coaching you before you enter into those anxiety filled situations that can make or break a project — or a career. Being able to think calmly and clearly in a variety of Global situations with all levels of management truly has been an asset to my career."
— *Jim Bartley, Director of North American Alliances, Whirlpool Corp., Benton Harbor, MI*

"In *SMART EMOTIONS*, Byron Stock takes you beyond simply learning about Emotional Intelligence to developing your Emotional Intelligence skills. The tools found in this book can have a profound effect on personal relationships, professional success, and physical well-being. You won't be disappointed!"
— *C. Randal Mullett, Vice President Government Relations and Public Affairs, Con-way Inc., Washington D.C.*

"Byron Stock is genius at making clear connections between emotional response and high performance in business. *SMART EMOTIONS* is a must-read competitive advantage for all who are looking to take their game to the next level!"
— *Patrick Chantelois, Senior Account Executive, Development Dimensions Intl., Southfield, MI*

"*SMART EMOTIONS* has given me the techniques to positively effect how I respond to my emotions. I blame myself less and find that I enjoy more peace and have enhanced my happiness at home and in my work. I strongly endorse *SMART EMOTIONS* to anyone interested in learning more about themselves and the physiology behind human emotions. Using these techniques, I now take the 'high road' and, through this, I am experiencing greater satisfaction and effectiveness in my life. This becomes powerful in the workplace since all work is done through relationships!"
— *Michael Tilbrooke, Regional Sales Director, Phoenix, AZ*

"With the techniques in *SMART EMOTIONS* I'm able to manage relationships better, reach decisions sooner, while maintaining everyone's dignity and creating feelings of inclusiveness."
— *Dr. Akinyinka Akinyele, former Lead Executive, US Government Agency, Chicago, IL*

"The physical benefits of using the techniques have been extraordinary — my blood pressure is down, I feel less stressed, and I am able to think more calmly and clearly."
— *Carolyn Thomas, Senior Director, US IT Business Solutions, McDonald's Corp., Oak Brook, IL*

"Emotional Intelligence is something I was completely unaware of in terms of being a tool that could help me in both my work and personal life. I understood the impact of my emotions on others, but didn't have the tools to harness them in a more positive, productive manner. After learning the techniques in *SMART EMOTIONS* I have found that emotions are a very powerful asset, and the ability to use the techniques to gain more positive outcomes has been a tremendous benefit. I highly recommend using the techniques in *SMART EMOTIONS* to anyone wanting to improve their lives and have positive control over their emotions."
— *Rick Golden, Strategic Business Consultant, Denver, CO*

"Excellent tools to learn and incorporate in everyday life, as well as enrich the lives of people you interact with, and improve bottom line results."
— *Karen Kramer, Global Accounts Manager, Seattle, WA*

"Prior to learning the Emotional Intelligence skills outlined in *SMART EMOTIONS*, I, like so many of us, often felt at the mercy of stress, whether it be the jitters before a presentation or a big meeting, sleepless nights in bed rehashing moments from the day, or coming home from work with a black cloud hanging over my head because of something that happened to me. While I can't say that these new skills have eliminated the stressful situations in my life, they sure have helped in my ability to deal with them — to quickly take command of how I'm feeling and choose a more healthy and useful emotion. *SMART EMOTIONS* gets right to the point without any hocus-pocus, and allows you to understand and use the science behind your emotions to take control and improve your life."
— *John Amrhein, Director of Finance, Holland, MI*

"The techniques that are taught by Byron Stock in *SMART EMOTIONS* really work! I've been using them since attending one of Byron's programs two years ago. They've helped me lead a better life — and do a better job in leading my organization. If you have an open mind about self improvement, you'll really benefit from Byron's wisdom."
— *John LaBrie, President, Con-way Freight, Ann Arbor, MI*

"The techniques I learned (and continue to use) have truly transformed my life, both professionally and privately. I've learned how to more effectively recognize and reframe my emotions in ways that are constructive, positive, and healthy. Open your heart and expand your life's fullness by reading and using the techniques in *SMART EMOTIONS*."
— *Sheila Thornton Warfield, Director Marketing Outreach, Zeeland, MI*

"I am amazed as to how decisions are effected by emotions, and even more amazed as to how these techniques help me find new solutions. I discovered that my emotions are a box confining my thoughts. Be ready — Byron gives the key to true "out of the box" thinking. Truly amazing when you look back on the changes it makes."
— *Liam Hickey, Director Facilities and Engineering, MPI Research, Mattawan, MI*

SMART EMOTIONS

For Busy Business People

> The "How To" book that teaches five simple techniques proven to increase resilience, personal productivity, and Emotional Intelligence skills.

Byron Stock

Copyright © 2008 by Byron Stock

All Rights Reserved. The reproduction of this work, or any portion thereof, in any form, by any electronic, mechanical, or other means, now known or here after invented, including xerography, photocopying, and recording and in any information storage and retrieval system, is forbidden without the written permission of Byron Stock & Associates LLC.

The material in this book, including the techniques, is intended for educational purposes only. It is not meant to take the place of diagnosis and treatment by a qualified medical practitioner or therapist. If you have any doubt about the suitability of any of these techniques for your personal use, please consult a licensed health care provider. No expressed or implied guarantee as to the effects of the use of the recommendations can be given nor liability taken.

While the examples and stories in this book are true, the names of individuals and organizations have been changed. Any similarities in these names are purely coincidental.

Requests for permission to use or reproduce material from this book should be directed to Permissions@ByronStock.com.

Library of Congress Cataloging-in-Publication Data

Stock, Byron, 1947-
SMART EMOTIONS for Busy Business People: The "How To" book that teaches five simple techniques proven to increase resilience, personal productivity, and Emotional Intelligence skills / Byron Stock.

ISBN 978-0-9802305-1-2
1. Business. 2. Self-help
I. Title

Byron Stock has been an Independent Certified Trainer for the HeartMath Inner Quality Management Program since 1995. His Emotional Intelligence program is an authorized derivative of that program. This book incorporates, with permission, techniques and concepts presented in the Inner Quality Management Program © 1996, Institute of HeartMath and ideas and recommendations by Jane Shuman of Shuman & Associates. SMART EMOTIONS, Developing Emotional Competence, Enhancing Personal Effectiveness, Developing Emotional Intelligence Skills, Building Resilience and Agility are trademarks of Byron Stock & Associates LLC. Inner Quality Management, Freeze-Frame, Heart Lock-In, and HeartMath are registered trademarks of the Institute of HeartMath. Intuitive Listening is a trademark of the Institute of HeartMath. The Freeze-Frame worksheet is adapted from HeartMath's Inner Quality Management workbook with permission of the Institute of HeartMath. All references to scientific research and reproduction of research materials used with permission of the Institute of HeartMath.

This book is dedicated to you, the reader.

I hope you use it to enhance your work and family life.

Table of Contents

Preface v

QUICK INFORMATION 1
    Is This Book For You? 1
    Decision Guide 1
    The SMART EMOTIONS Map 2
    Emotional Intelligence Skills 3
    Benefits of Increasing Your Emotional Intelligence Skills 5
    How SMART EMOTIONS Is Unique 7

CHAPTER 1 — EMOTIONAL INTELLIGENCE 11
    What is Emotional Intelligence? 11
    The Importance of Emotional Intelligence At Work And At Home 17
    The Science Of Emotional Intelligence 29

CHAPTER 2 — PREPARATION 47
    What Will Make You Successful? 47
    Selecting Your Personal Goals 48
    Peer Coaching 56

CHAPTER 3 — SKILL-BUILDING TECHNIQUES 63
    Technique #1 — What Am I Feeling Right Now? 63
    Technique #2 — Freeze-Frame® 74
    Technique #3 — Appreciation 92
    Technique #4 — Heart Lock-In® 103
    Technique #5 — Intuitive Listening™ 114

CHAPTER 4 — RESULTS 129
    Illustrative Stories 129
    Clients' Comments For Each Technique 139
    Clients' Comments for Each Personal Goal 145
    Data 162

ABOUT THE AUTHOR 172
ACKNOWLEDGEMENTS.. 173
REFERENCES 176
ADDITIONAL BOOKS ON EMOTIONAL INTELLIGENCE 177
BOOKS FROM HEARTMATH 178
INDEX 179
LEADER'S GUIDE FOR SMART EMOTIONS 186
TRAINING PROGRAMS, SEMINARS, AND WORKSHOPS 188

PREFACE

In 1995 I attended a seminar at the Institute of HeartMath in California. The Institute's learning center is situated on about 100 acres in the mountains between San Jose and Santa Cruz. The setting is peace-filled and beautiful. On the third day of the seminar we were told there would be a reception in the evening. The founder of the Institute, Doc Childre, would be there. The staff of the Institute hold Doc in very high regard, and because of his busy schedule, he rarely had time to attend evening events with seminar participants. I was impressed with the techniques he had created and was excited to have the opportunity to speak with him, and more importantly, to ask questions and learn from him.

In one of our small group sessions that day, I made the statement that I didn't know what I wanted to ask Doc. This was an opportunity that didn't occur often, and I wanted to take full advantage of hearing his thoughts on questions I had. Upon hearing me say this, Quan Lee, a young man from Taiwan, asked if he could tell me a story:

> One evening, Firefly was busy flying about when he looked up in the dark night sky and saw Miss Moon. "Oh Miss Moon, how beautiful you are! Your light is so bright. I wish my light was as bright and beautiful as you!" Miss Moon looked down and replied, "Thank you Firefly, but I think your light is more beautiful than mine." Firefly responded, "Oh no, you are so big and so bright, you are the most beautiful." Miss Moon looked down on little Firefly. "Firefly, you are most beautiful. My light comes from the sun; your light comes from within." *(Note: source unknown)*

Quan Lee looked at me and said, "Byron, you are like Firefly. You have a light within you. Don't be afraid to share it."

So now, having been encouraged by people who attended my programs and by my friends, colleagues, and family, I've written this book.

It is *not* what some of my close friends would expect, because they know I can talk forever on the subject of Emotional Intelligence and can share hundreds of stories participants in our development programs have told me.

This book does not contain information on subjects such as the history of Emotional Intelligence and its founders; alternative definitions and views of its competencies; survey assessment instruments and a long list of others. It is not that these subjects aren't interesting; they are. In fact, they illustrate how many of our life situations are impacted by our mismanaged emotions. It's just that you don't need to know all that information to develop *your* Emotional Intelligence skills. If you want to learn about those things, there are at least 25 other books you can read on the subject of Emotional Intelligence.

I have no desire to produce "just another book" on Emotional Intelligence. I am very clear on my purpose in writing this book and what I expect it to accomplish. **SMART EMOTIONS** concentrates on simple, basic "how to" techniques with the *minimal* amount of background information you'll need to develop your Emotional Intelligence skills. "How to" books such as this one should be efficient and should demonstrate, through their content and layout, sincere care for the readers. Drawing on years of practical experience helping thousands of people, we know what works and what doesn't.

If you want to learn simple, proven techniques that will improve your life, **SMART EMOTIONS** is the book for you!

QUICK INFORMATION

IS THIS BOOK FOR YOU?

SMART EMOTIONS has been written with you in mind. You are beyond busy. You don't have time for things that are not obviously and immediately relevant and useful in your professional and personal life. So there is no more description or detail or explanation than what you actually need in order to learn and practice the techniques. You won't invest any more of your precious time and energy than necessary to receive the significant benefits this book has for you.

DECISION GUIDE

Whenever you make a purchase decision about a book, there are informal criteria you use to decide whether or not the book will truly be of benefit to you. Unfortunately, most books do not provide that information in an organized, succinct format.

SMART EMOTIONS makes it easy for you. Simply look down the "I want to see…" column below to identify those criteria important to you. Then turn to the page listed and read as little or as much as you need to determine whether this book will be of value to you.

Decision Guide

I Want to See …	Page
• An overall "map" of how the book is organized	2
• What Emotional Intelligence is (definition)	3
• The benefits of increasing my Emotional Intelligence skills	5
• The techniques that will build your skills	63
• What you can improve by practicing the techniques	49
• The science behind Emotional Intelligence	29
• Results and data from use of the techniques	129
• Emotional Intelligence competencies	12
• The impact on teams and organizations	162
• What makes this book unique	7
• Comments from others who use the techniques	139
• Coaching support (Chapter 3 — end of each technique)	71
• Free resources to support you	8

THE SMART EMOTIONS MAP

The **SMART EMOTIONS** Map is a reference tool that shows how this book is organized. The Background is just that, background information that may be of interest in learning about Emotional Intelligence. It is not necessary to read this section to develop your skills.

**Figure 1.
The SMART EMOTIONS Map**

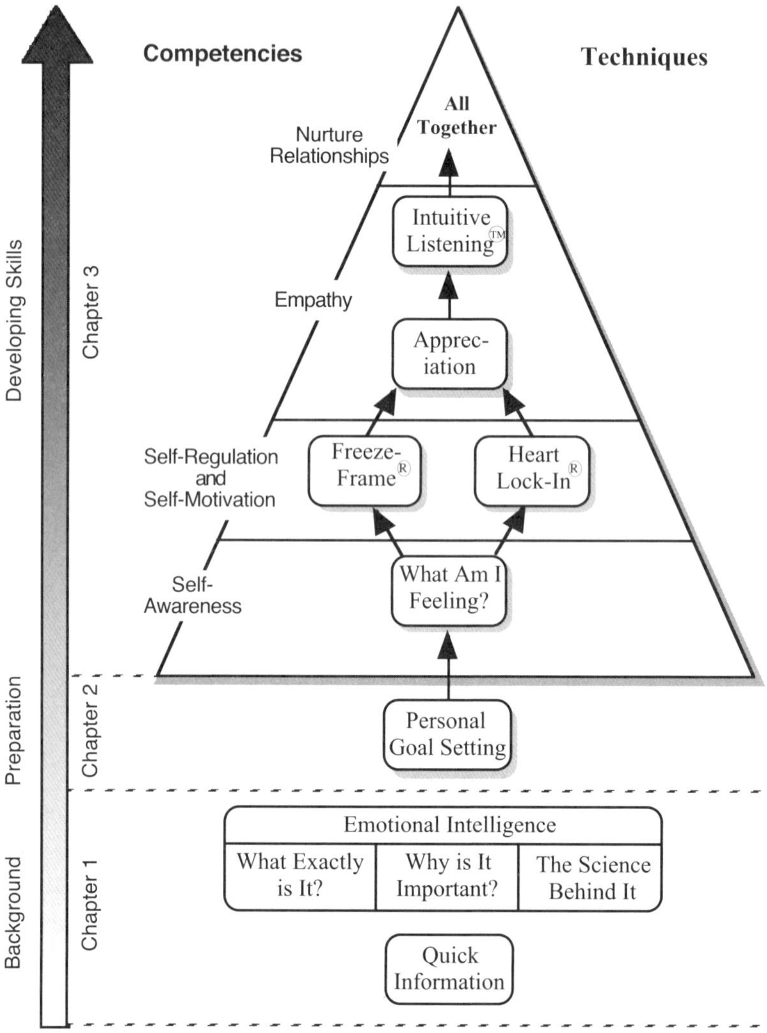

Freeze-Frame and Heart Lock-In are registered trademarks and Intuitive Listening is a trademark of the Institute of HeartMath.

The Preparation work is an important section because it guides you in selecting your Personal Goals — what you want to improve. In Chapter 3 you will learn and practice the five specific techniques that develop your Emotional Intelligence skills.

Your Emotional Intelligence

Emotional Intelligence (EI) is your ability (natural or learned) to acquire and apply knowledge from your emotions and the emotions of others. The purpose of developing skill in using your Emotional Intelligence is to help you make better decisions about what to say and what to do (or not say and do). Like other intelligences we need to develop, such as mathematical, linguistic and spatial, Emotional Intelligence enables us to make good decisions and manage our lives so we are happy and fulfilled.

A key word in the definition above is "ability." Ability indicates you can improve if you practice. All you have to be taught is "how to do it" to begin to get better. To continue to improve, of course you must then practice "doing it!"

> **"Ability" indicates you can do it if you practice. All you have to be taught is how.**

The Need for Emotional Intelligence Skills

The pressures people are experiencing in business and government to do more... with less... faster... better... cheaper... are taking an increasing toll on performance, health, and relationships. The stress has grown steadily over the past 15–20 years. You read and hear the statistics almost daily. You know stress affects you — and others. You see it in others and experience it yourself every day.

Stress is a result of negative emotions (fear, frustration, anxiety, embarrassment, shock, worry, etc.) and beliefs that occur when people feel unable to deal with the demands of their environment. And the demands of both work and family environments have been increasing almost exponentially. In the description of stress above, the word "unable" is key; *not possessing the skill of managing one's emotions.*

A Vice President of Product Development of a large manufacturing company participating in our skill-development program expressed concern that companies are putting their workers in jeopardy. "The levels of stress and the pace of work are not sustainable, even in the short term," she said. A director in her company told her that as they walked out of a meeting, one of the attendees said to him in all seriousness, "Will you come to my funeral?"

At home things aren't much better. You come home from work exhausted, only to remember the children need to be taken to a whole host of activities. Some of these activities are social, some physical. Some are important in developing interests and skills that may be valuable to your children's future. Later, you may find yourself helping with homework,

> **Stress occurs when people feel unable to deal with the demands of their environment. The word "unable" is key:** *not possessing the skill of managing one's emotions.*

feeling the stress your kids are feeling to learn more, quicker. Finally, after taking care of the children, you get to sit down, read the mail, pay the bills — and in many cases, get on the computer to answer emails or get work done that you didn't find time for earlier.

Mismanaged Emotions

Stress from mismanaged emotions impacts every area of a person's life. It shows up in individuals as:

- lack of mental clarity
- poor performance
- poor decision-making
- poor communication
- ineffective leadership
- migraine headaches
- digestive problems
- heart arrhythmia
- panic attacks
- interrupting others
- depression
- memory loss
- conflict with others
- lack of teamwork
- sleeplessness
- high blood pressure
- poor work/life balance
- family turmoil

The impact of mismanaged emotions on organizations and their people reads like a list of typical issues (problems) faced by almost every organization:

- lower productivity
- turnover
- decreased loyalty
- poor quality
- losing high-performers
- "us - them" behavior
- product problems
- customer complaints
- loss of customer loyalty
- reduced margins
- late change deployment
- poor work climate

Every day you went to school you invested roughly an hour a day, five days a week, nine months a year for eight to twelve years to develop your skills in math, reading, writing, languages and others — skills that are important to enable you to manage yourself and make good decisions about your life.

You, like most of us, probably did not invest time in skill-building specific, focused, training in grade school, high school or college in recognizing and regulating your emotions. Therein lies the gaping hole in our educational system. Virtually every one of us can benefit from learning how to improve our Emotional Intelligence skills.

BENEFITS OF INCREASING YOUR EMOTIONAL INTELLIGENCE SKILLS

What Can You Expect to Gain?
If you experience negative emotions and feelings at work or at home, **SMART EMOTIONS** will show you how to recognize and transform those negative, draining feelings into positive, productive emotions and action. You can use the five simple, proven techniques to develop your Emotional Intelligence skills and increase your resilience, performance and mental clarity. Based on published scientific research, the Institute of HeartMath techniques have proven effective for over 15 years (The Institute of HeartMath, *Research Overview*). They have helped people from all walks of life who work in all types of organizations in the United States, Canada, Sweden, England, Thailand, Australia, Taiwan and around the world.

Simply put, these techniques work. They work for people like you, and for the people who report directly to you, in business, government or non-profits. They will also work for your spouse, teenaged children, colleagues and friends. Using the techniques in this book will make your life at work and at home significantly better — forever!

There's just one catch! To experience dramatic improvements in your life, it is absolutely necessary to make a commitment to take a few seconds every day to use and practice the techniques. Skill development comes from "doing," not just reading.

The Benefits
Increasing your Emotional Intelligence skills offers benefits in three categories: decision-making, relationships, and health. These categories embrace virtually every behavior, every action and reaction, every situation you may encounter. They apply to your business and professional interactions as well as your family relationships, from the broad sweep of major, multi-million dollar corporations to the day-to-day small incidents that influence your life.

> **Decision Making** By becoming aware of what you are feeling *in-the-moment* you have information you can use to make a decision about what to say or do *now*. By developing emotional self-regulation skills you can quickly transform out of negative, draining emotions into more positive, productive ones, enabling you to think and act more rationally at any time. Your moment-to-moment decision-making is enhanced significantly. You can use these skills to keep yourself from reacting, allowing you to respond with more thoughtfulness and thoroughness.

Being in control of your emotions has a huge positive impact on your performance, your effectiveness, your confidence and your motivation.

Relationships Emotional Intelligence skills will not only empower you personally; they will have a positive impact on your relationships with others as well. For example, instead of blowing up when your project manager announces a deadline without consulting you, managing your emotional reactiveness enables you to remain calm, ask good questions, perhaps even influence the deadline — all the while preserving your good working relationship with your manager.

On the home front, when your child comes home with a poor test score or lower grade than you think he can earn, rather than putting him on the hot seat, you can show him you care and are concerned about him, and still maintain a firm but understanding approach to the situation. Think of the positive effect this is likely to have on your relationships with your children.

Health The third area affected by developing your Emotional Intelligence skills, but certainly not the least, is your health. Negative emotions fuel higher cortisol levels, often called "the stress hormone." Over time, excessive levels of cortisol can cause sleeplessness, loss of bone mass and osteoporosis, allergies, asthma, acid reflux, ulcers, low sperm count, redistribution of fat to the waist and hips, and fat buildup in the arteries, which can lead to heart disease and numerous other diseases (McCraty, Borrios-Choplin et al.). Mismanaged emotions, correlated with dysrhythmias in our Autonomic Nervous System, are associated with many diseases including asthma, chronic fatigue, depression, hypoglycemia, hypertension and many more. Learning to transform from negative emotions into positive productive ones throughout the day or night over a sustained period of time has been shown to have a positive impact on many health-related problems. The most frequently mentioned by participants in my programs is a significant reduction or elimination of sleeplessness, often in one or two weeks.

HOW SMART EMOTIONS IS UNIQUE

Several factors make **SMART EMOTIONS** unique among other books about Emotional Intelligence. You will find in these pages, presented in practical, simple usable steps:

1. The "SMART EMOTIONS Map" This "map" serves as a visual to show how the book is organized. It can serve as a reference to help you decide what you want to read and to let you know how you're progressing through the book.

2. Five Simple Techniques to Develop Emotional Competencies There are five techniques that specifically address the five emotional competencies you need to develop for successful living. Each technique is presented and explained in a format you can learn and practice with ease. You can rely on our experience in helping hundreds of people just like you, since 1995.

3. A Way to Identify Your Needs This book enables you to identify what you want to improve through the 17 Personal Goals in Chapter 2, and then shows you in the Personal Goals/Techniques Matrix which techniques you can use to experience improvement.

4. Immediate Help for Your Specific Situations We read books because we believe they will benefit us in some way. The Personal Goal-Setting activity (Chapter 2) enables you to list specific situations you are experiencing in which the techniques can be used to help you immediately.

5. "Doing," Not Just "Knowing" One of the most beneficial learnings from studies and applications of instructional design or training principles is the need to ask the right questions. In this case the first question is, "What do you want to be able to *do* as a result of reading and using this book?" The second question then follows, "What is the minimum content you need to *know* in order to do it?"

SMART EMOTIONS concentrates on teaching you techniques ("Doing") and provides only the amount of "Knowing" material required for you to effectively put the "Doing" into practice. This is an efficient and caring approach to increasing your Emotional Intelligence skills.

6. Examples of Real Business Situations Near the beginning of each technique in Chapter 3 is a listing of typical situations where that technique could effectively be utilized. This will make it easy for you to see when a technique is appropriate to your needs. The participant stories and comments in Chapter 4 provide additional specific, real situations to help you learn how others have used the techniques.

7. Practice Pages and Samples Using the practice pages and reading the samples enable you to focus, relate, and connect with the material. All the practice pages are focused on helping you identify and relate to your own actual situations and experiences.

8. Coaching Thousands of face-to-face and phone-coaching sessions have been analyzed to identify the typical difficulties people experience in applying each of the techniques. At the end of each technique are listed typical difficulties and suggested solutions that have proven to be helpful in that specific area.

9. How Others Have Benefited It's helpful to know how people like you have used and benefited from these techniques. Included in this book are four resources that will bring the techniques and their application to life:
   A. Situations in which clients have used specific techniques are described at the beginning of each section in Chapter 3
   B. Illustrative stories: Chapter 4
   C. Benefits of using the techniques are listed by technique or personal goal: Chapter 4
   D. Results data: Chapter 4

10. Free Resources
Weekly Email   It is important to be supported as you learn and apply the techniques. You may choose to receive a free, weekly email reminder from our office. These emails contain a short reminder to use one technique each week, along with a positive inspirational quote. They do not contain any "marketing" material. People often tell us these reminders are the only positive email they ever receive! Request the email at http://www.ByronStock.com/resources.html.
  Your name and email address will not be sold or provided to other organizations.

Reminder Stickers help you remember to use what you have learned. From our website you can download an electronic file of reminder stickers and print the file on a standard sheet of 1" x 2" adhesive labels (http://www.ByronStock.com/resources .html). These stickers are a simple, low-tech way to increase your likelihood of remembering to use the techniques.

One Man's Story

Chet's story traces the progress of just one individual as he moved through the steps of the program, putting each technique to work as he gained skill and experience.

The Challenge: To create a new international team who would influence key persons in the company's 30,000 worldwide locations to adopt or use new software and procedures. Chet wanted a team who could listen to the clients' concerns and ensure they had input on the software and how it could better meet their needs. They would be responsible for presenting the clients' recommendations to the Information Technology (IT) executives who would make the decisions. The stress would be considerable.

The Gift: A 43-year-old senior director of IT for a global company in the U.S., Chet met his new international team for the first time at our Emotional Intelligence development program. His objectives for his team were both professional and personal. He wanted to give them the gift of proven techniques to improve their influencing skills, help with the demands of their jobs and reduce their stress to increase their quality of life.

The First Step — Setting Personal Goals: In his first personal interview, Chet selected the following goals:

1. To learn to "Listen More and Talk Less" in his job and at home.
   Chet felt he was too quick to give his opinion, too opinionated.
2. To "Increase Personal Productivity."
   Chet felt frustrated by too many commitments. He always had work thoughts on his mind, causing him restless sleep.
3. To "Gain Greater Mental Clarity."
   Sleeplessness, along with Chet's travel schedule, led to a lack of focus. Although he had a very strategic mind, he felt he didn't organize strategy as well or as succinctly as he desired.

Immediate Follow-Through: Chet's team all participated in the Emotional Intelligence development program that was his gift to them, and practiced applying the techniques to their own situations. They met for their first planning meeting the day after the training ended.

Follow-up Coaching: One week later, Chet was seeing significant improvement in his work and his personal life. He was catching his negative thoughts and switching them to positive ones, getting fewer negative responses. He was now able to go right to sleep and not wake up with work thoughts on his mind, producing increased energy and mental clarity. In his performance review with his boss, he heard the boss out, stayed calm and asked follow-up questions, and received the most helpful feedback he had heard in 23 years.

Second Coaching, Three Weeks Later: The second coaching session found Chet continuing to improve. He gave several examples of how using the techniques was helping him achieve his own personal goals as well as helping the company. Following a presentation to several IT vice presidents, in which he relied on skills he had acquired, his boss reported receiving very high praise about Chet from a VP with whom Chet had previously not had a particularly comfortable relationship.

"Impact Interview," Two Months Later: Chet gave more examples of how use of the techniques had helped him to influence senior leaders. He spoke of how happy he was because of the real heart connection he was creating at home. His team members were also experiencing significant benefits, enabling them to be ahead of scheduled implementation of the software systems.

One Year Later: In preparation for training another of Chet's groups, he shared with me dramatic improvements in Employee Commitment scores that his first group had attained. While the other group had negligible improvement, Chet's group's overall score had jumped from the mid 70s to the high 80s. The only explanation he had was that he and his team were all using the Emotional Intelligence techniques.

> *Chet's story is representative of many we hear when people learn the techniques presented in this book. It illustrates the many benefits available to individuals who enhance their Emotional Intelligence skills.*

CHAPTER 1

EMOTIONAL INTELLIGENCE

In the three sections of this chapter you'll learn:
What is Emotional Intelligence?
- What Emotional Intelligence is and is not.
- The core competencies of Emotional Intelligence.

The Importance of Emotional Intelligence at Work and Home
- The impact of emotions on leadership, culture and values, stress, health, change effectiveness, customer service and more.
- Sample results that can be achieved by applying and practicing the techniques taught in this book.

The Science of Emotional Intelligence
- The significant impact of emotions on the Autonomic Nervous System.
- The impact of emotions on our other biological systems and on "dis-eases" within the body.
- The impact of positive and negative emotions on health.
- Ways in which your heart impacts your brain and the quality of your thinking.
- How your "emotional brain" can keep you from thinking clearly.
- The impact of your emotions on your heart rhythms.

Section I
WHAT IS EMOTIONAL INTELLIGENCE?

There are a variety of definitions of Emotional Intelligence, depending on which book you read. Ours is very simple:

> *Emotional Intelligence is your ability, natural or learned, to acquire and apply knowledge from your emotions and the emotions of others.*

The purpose of developing our Emotional Intelligence is to help us make better decisions about what to say or do — or not say or do.

This basic format for defining intelligence can be applied to any intelligence. For example, mathematical intelligence:

> **Mathematical intelligence** *is your ability, natural or learned, to acquire and apply knowledge from figures and symbols.*

Or, **linguistic intelligence**: *your ability to read, write and understand what others are saying.*

We develop mathematical or linguistic intelligence, or any of the other skills we went to school for, to help us make better decisions about what to do. Unfortunately, few, if any of us, were given opportunities to work with our Emotional Intelligence skills as we grew up. All of us can benefit tremendously by recognizing and putting into practice the knowledge we gain from our emotions and the emotions of others.

The Five Emotional Intelligence Competencies

In the literature on the subject of Emotional Intelligence, you will find lists of widely varying numbers of emotional competencies, some as many as twenty.

SMART EMOTIONS is focused on five basic emotional competencies you can develop to use your emotions more effectively (Goleman pg. 43):
1. Emotional Self-Awareness
2. Emotional Self-Regulation
3. Emotional Self-Motivation
4. Empathy
5. Nurturing Relationships

**Figure 2.
The Five Emotional Competencies Developed
Through Techniques in This Book**

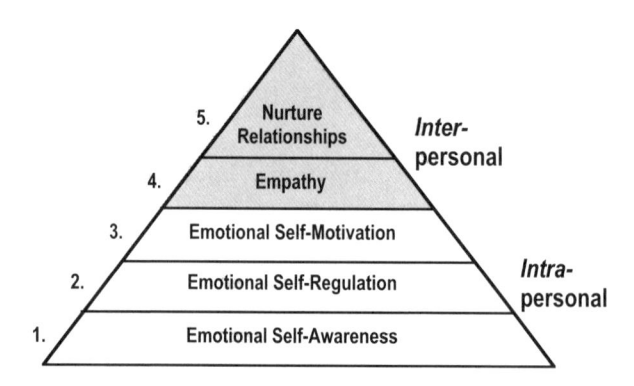

A Self-Check of Emotions

A good way to see the impact of your emotions on yourself is to check your awareness of your emotions. Think about the following: in the past year have you felt anxious, frustrated, annoyed, irritated or angry? How about in the past month? In the past 24 hours? How about in the past hour? Now ask yourself if those emotions have caused you or others you interact with any of the following: stress, time wasted worrying, rigidity of position, conflict, ineffective communication, headaches, sleepless nights, muscle tension, or other physical problems? You probably answered "yes" to one or more of these effects of negative emotions.

Negative Emotions Affect Your Ability to...
- get your work done
- resolve conflicts constructively
- manage change effectively
- lead others
- communicate clearly
- influence others
- maintain your health
- enjoy your life

Mismanaged Emotions Are also a Major Factor in...
- absenteeism
- customer dissatisfaction
- employee turnover
- poor decision-making
- low employee engagement
- employee dissatisfaction
- goal attainment
- "silo" mentality
- poor teamwork
- low trust/loyalty
- grievances
- healthcare costs
- patient safety
- "politics"
- inefficient problem solving
- poor project management
- quality problems
- vendor relations
- work/life balance
- workplace violence

Emotions impact every moment of your life and are an important part of what determines your performance and your quality of life. That is why you will want to develop your emotional self-awareness and management skills.

The Intrapersonal Competencies
The first three Emotional Intelligence competencies, emotional self-awareness, emotional self-regulation, and emotional self-motivation, constitute an *intra*personal set of skills.

The intrapersonal skills are internal, unseen. The more effective we become in these foundational intrapersonal skills, the easier it will be to develop skills in the other competencies. When you manage your emotions more effectively, you'll interact more easily and effectively with others.

1. Emotional Self-Awareness The competency at the bottom of the pyramid is Emotional Self-Awareness. This is the foundation competency. It has to do with being aware of *what* you're feeling in-the-moment. The key word here is "what," not "how." Ask someone "how" he is feeling and he will typically say "fine." Unfortunately, "fine" is a grade of sandpaper, not an emotion. "What" is the better word, because it requires the naming of an emotion. If you don't know what emotion you're feeling, you don't have the information you need to decide whether to stay in the emotion or to change it.

Have you ever been around someone who isn't aware of his or her emotions, particularly negative ones? What's that like for you? Do you want to work with that person? What's the impact on teamwork? What's the impact on you and your work? What's the impact on that person and on his or her career? Emotional Self-Awareness is the first skill you will learn to develop in Chapter 3.

2. Emotional Self-Regulation The second Emotional Intelligence competency is Emotional Self-Regulation. This is not about "stuffing, holding in, or hiding" our emotions; rather it is about being able to choose our emotions. The key word is to "transform" our emotions. If we don't like the emotion we're experiencing, it would be beneficial if we were able to choose a better one, or transform it into a more positive, productive emotion.

3. Emotional Self-Motivation The third Emotional Intelligence competency is Emotional Self-Motivation. This is about having the skill to activate positive, productive emotions. Frequently, people who have ascended to high positions in organizations or who are top performers in their professional field are very good at this. They are able to stay optimistic and enthusiastic about projects they have to complete, difficulties they have to deal with, and people whose opinions and views do not align with their own. The two key words associated with this competency are persistence and success. Our ability to call up and use positive emotions such as excitement, enthusiasm, joy, courage, etc., is critical to self-motivation.

The Interpersonal Competencies

The interpersonal skills are empathy and nurturing relationships.

4. Empathy The fourth Emotional Intelligence competency is empathy. Empathy should not be confused with sympathy. Empathy is the ability to put yourself in "someone else's shoes" so you can see the situation from their point-of-view. It doesn't mean you have to agree with them. By putting ourselves in someone else's shoes, we not only learn and understand how they feel, we can also use that information to help us adjust our position or approach to arrive at win-win solutions to disagreements or conflicts.

The Senior VP of Human Resources of a company shared this experience:

> The first Monday of every month the CEO gathered a group of about 300 employees together for 30 minutes to provide an update on the business. One Monday morning, he walked in, head down, with a rather sad and bewildered look on his face. As he approached the microphone, he nervously adjusted his tie, looked out at his people, looked down at his notes and began to read, "As of eight o'clock this morning we were purchased by the Paragon Corporation."
>
> People in the audience stared in disbelief. Feelings of fear and concern showed on their faces. He looked out at the audience bleakly. People in the audience looked at each other in bewilderment. He then looked back down at his notes. After what seemed like an eternity, he looked up and said, "I have a correction to make. As of eight o'clock this morning *we purchased* the Paragon Company. I wanted you to know exactly what those people are feeling right now. I want you to keep in mind the feelings you just had as you work with the people from Paragon."
>
> Over the next few weeks and months as discussions were held about integrating Paragon and its people into the organization, questions were frequently raised about how the proposed changes would affect the feelings of the Paragon people. The sincere compassion and empathy exhibited was an important factor in a smooth acquisition and integration.

5. Nurturing Relationships The fifth Emotional Intelligence competency is nurturing relationships, "setting a positive tone of cooperation," even if things aren't going well. In times of difficulty, rather than trying to regulate other people's emotions, we must be able to manage our own in order to have authentic concern or care for others and ourselves. This fifth competency is available to you once you learn how to use and apply the techniques in the other four competencies.

A good example comes from an interview with the Chief Learning Officer of a large energy company:

Recently, the organization acquired another company. At that time, there were a total of 28 people in her department. The other company had 34 people in a similar department. Her CEO told her she could keep half of the total combined number.

She talked with the CEO to make sure she understood his strategic agenda. From that, she determined the skills, abilities, and talents she needed in her department to support his strategies. With this information, she then reviewed each individual's work history, resume, and performance record. She talked with each person's immediate supervisor to find out about strengths, weaknesses, competencies, and talents. By matching the information, she selected the people who had the skills and experience she required.

One at a time, she brought each person who would not be retained into her office and explained exactly why they were to be let go. She carefully explained the process she had used to make her decisions, and offered to write letters or make personal phone calls to help them get another job.

From the time she had the one-to-one discussions to the time the people actually left the company, there was about a two-month period. During that time, people told her they were happy to be working for her even though they were leaving. One said, "The reason everyone is working so hard is, we know you really care about us."

This is an excellent example of applying the Emotional Intelligence competencies to create a "positive tone of cooperation" even when things weren't going well.

Emotional Intelligence is About a Different Way of Being Smart

In summary, Emotional Intelligence is not about being soft. It means being intelligent about our emotions — a different way of being smart. That is, having the emotional management skills to be more effective *in-the-moment*! This book will teach you the techniques to develop your Emotional Intelligence skills.

Section II
THE IMPORTANCE OF EMOTIONAL INTELLIGENCE AT WORK AND HOME

Leaders, Employees, Customers and the Bottom Line

The emotions that leaders, employees, and customers feel impact the bottom line of companies and the effectiveness of government and non-profit organizations. The emotions that leaders experience impact the climate and culture of an organization as a whole. More specifically, leaders' emotions impact:
- What employees feel
- How satisfied employees are with their work and the company
- How loyal they are and their willingness to give extra effort
- How productive and efficient they are.

Figure 3.
Leaders, Employees, Customers, and the Bottom Line

Profitability
↑
Customers
↑
Employees
↑
Leaders

How employees feel and perform their work impact how customers feel, how satisfied they are with both products and services, and ultimately how loyal a customer is to the company or organization. And how loyal customers are has a direct impact on the bottom line and profitability of an organization.

Notice that the foundation element in this set of relationships is leadership. It does not say CEO or Executive Vice President or Director. It says leaders. The in-charge person in every work team, every manager, and every individual in the organization is a leader. Self-leadership is one of the most important factors we focus on in skill development. Self-leadership is the internal ability to lead *yourself* to make the best choices and decisions moment-to-moment throughout the day, whether at work or at home.

The Impact of Emotions of Leaders, Employees, and Customers

Both positive and negative emotions impact everyone in organizations and the customers they serve. The figure below depicts the impact of negative emotions on all of the people and the bottom line.

**Figure 4.
Some of the Problems Caused by Mismanaged or Unmanaged Emotions**

Profitability
- Decreased profitability
- Reduced margins

Customers
- Customer defection
- Customer dissatisfaction
- Customer complaints
- Anti-company web sites
- Distributor pushback
- Lawsuits

Employees
- Errors and mistakes
- Poor performance
- High stress
- Lack of adaptability
- Poor attitudes
- Low morale
- Communication gaps
- Lack of initiative
- Lack of trust
- Increased conflict
- Resistance to change
- Quality problems
- Lack of teamwork
- Decreased loyalty
- Health problems
- Turnover
- Low work/life balance

Leaders
- Negative climate
- Ineffective self-leadership
- Poor role model
- Bad Decisions

The following specific research and examples support and demonstrate how Emotional Intelligence skills — or the lack of them — impact every person, process, and outcome in companies, government agencies, and non-profit organizations.

Emotions and Leadership

In "What Makes a Leader?" in the *Harvard Business Review*, Daniel Goleman states, "When I calculated the ratio of technical skills, IQ, and Emotional Intelligence as ingredients of excellent performance, Emotional Intelligence proved to be twice as important as the others for jobs at all levels." He goes on to say, "When I compared star performers with average ones in senior leadership positions, nearly 90% of the difference in their profiles was attributable to Emotional Intelligence factors rather than cognitive abilities." Note that he did not say that IQ or technical skills are not important. They are. These important capacities simply get us in the door. From there, whether or not we are highly productive in the organization or move up is largely determined by how well we manage our emotions and relate to and interact with other people.

Goleman goes on to say, "... when senior managers had a critical mass of Emotional Intelligence capabilities, their divisions outperformed the yearly earnings goals by 20%. Division leaders without that critical mass underperformed by about the same amount." Developing our Emotional Intelligence skills is critical to self-leadership and leadership of others — and to the bottom line.

Additional Support
In *Primal Leadership*, Daniel Goleman, Richard Boyatsis, and Annie McKee cite the following: "The study found the more positive the overall moods (emotions) of people in the top management team, the more cooperatively they worked together — and the better the company's results." They also state, "In a study of 19 insurance companies, the climate created by the CEO's among their direct reports predicted the business performance of the entire organization; in 75% of cases, climate alone accurately sorted companies into high versus low profit and growth." Organizational climate is a function of the perception of people about the organization and its leaders, which is directly attributed to the leadership and management style of the leaders.

Other leading business researchers and authors including James Koznes and Barry Posner, authors of *The Leadership Challenge*, support the importance of Emotional Intelligence. In their paper, "The Best Learning Practices of the Best Leaders," they cite tips for effective leadership. The number one tip is to be self-aware. "There's solid evidence that the best leaders are highly attuned to what's going on inside of them as they're leading. They're very self-aware. They're also quite aware of the impact they're having on others. In fact, self-awareness may be the most crucial learning skill of all." The second tip is to manage our emotions. "While the best leaders are self-aware, they're careful not to let their feelings manage them. Instead, they manage their feelings."

Organizational Culture and Values
Organizational culture is an amalgam of behaviors, values, and beliefs that together create the climate and "feel" of an organization. Analysts who examine and evaluate organizations are recognizing this important element of organizations. Marcus Buckingham, author of *First Break All The Rules,* was quoted in a January 2003 *Fast Company* magazine article "Idea Fest," "We're just beginning to realize how economically valuable emotions are, and it's clear they're largely out of control. Analysts had even started to downgrade companies... whose cultures, they believe, are eroding, even if their earnings

are holding up." Although it may seem obvious, research verifies that how we behave, how we treat others and the resulting emotions employees feel has a long-term impact on the profitability of a company.

Attitudes Impact Revenue

In an elaborate 800-store study by Sears, Roebuck and Company reported in the *Wall Street Journal* article "Companies Are Finding It Really Pays to Be Nice to Employees," support for the validity of how leaders affect employees can be seen. Sears found, "...if employee attitudes improve by 5%, customer satisfaction will jump 1.3%, driving a one half-percentage point rise in revenue." If people *feel* better about how they're treated, they satisfy customers more effectively which, in turn, will impact the bottom line.

Stress

It is obvious that stress has an impact on both leaders and employees. Stress is the result of negative emotions and beliefs that occur whenever people feel unable to cope with the demands from their environment. The three key words in this definition of stress are *emotions, unable*, and *demands*. The *demands* of our work and our social settings are not likely to decrease in the future. Since that is the case, it makes sense to develop skills so we are more able to deal with the negative *emotions* those *demands* place on us.

How Emotions Impact Performance

At some point, each of us will reach a peak in our performance curve when we perceive we are at our capacity. When we reach this peak, a little voice in our head starts mumbling phrases like, "I don't think I can get this all done," and "What's going to happen to me if I don't?"

Figure 5.
Healthy and Unhealthy Impact of Challenge and Its Effects on Performance

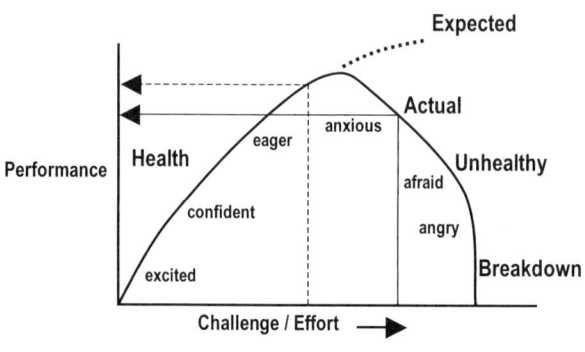

Adapted from the Institute of HeartMath

Anxiety, fear, and even despair can enter into our mind. We become defensive and start looking out for our own security. We get frustrated and angry when one of our colleagues doesn't provide us with the information we need to complete our project. As a result our performance declines (see solid line arrow in the above figure). It is important to note here that our relevant experience hasn't changed, our IQ hasn't changed, and our technical expertise hasn't changed. What has changed is our emotional mood! That's what is hampering our performance! You'll learn more about the physiology that causes this to happen in the Science section of Chapter 1.

Good Stress and Bad Stress
On the left side of the peak of the performance curve is what's referred to as "good stress" or "*eustress*," which is fueled by positive emotions and optimism. On the right side of the peak is what's called "bad stress," fueled by negative, often unmanaged emotions. Stress is an internal reaction, or negative emotion, to an external event. Without the skills to manage our emotions, our performance is likely to decline as we are expected to do more and more. Stress, good or bad, has to do with the emotions being experienced and how those emotions affect performance.

Health
There is a relationship between our emotions and our health. A study that cites the impact of mismanaged emotions can be found in the *British Journal of Medical Psychology,* "Personality, Stress and Cancer: Prediction and Prophylaxis." It states, "Emotional stress was more predictive of death from cancer and cardiovascular disease than smoking: people who were unable to effectively manage their stress had a 40% higher death rate than more emotionally managed individuals."

Managing Emotions Improves Performance
By being aware of our emotions and being able to manage them by choosing the emotions we want to experience, we can maintain — and even improve — our peak performance. Take the same situation in which we're feeling overwhelmed and overloaded, feeling anxious, afraid, scared, worried and even angry. What can be done to change this situation? Following is a real life example of what can happen.

Figure 6.
Impact of Increased Emotional Self-Management on Performance

Adapted from the Institute of HeartMath

In the fall of 2005, I conducted our applied Emotional Intelligence skill-building program for a group of high potential (Hi-Pos) people who work for a large manufacturing company. I provided the program to the first group on a Tuesday and Wednesday and scheduled my first coaching session with each person the following week. Monday morning I received the following email from one of the participants:

> *"I had been having an extremely stressful week last week — with a crushing, impending feeling of failure/doom that I wasn't going to be able to get everything done to meet some very important deadlines. Since your course, I've been using all of the techniques and am AMAZED how successful they have been. I've been able to 'get on top of' everything that needs to get done with little to no agitation. You very well may have helped me with one of the most significant positive improvements I've ever made in my life — I'm hopeful that success will continue."*

What had this person accomplished? He had shifted his stress curve up and to the right, resulting in improved performance. In a very short time, by applying the techniques, he was able to transform the negative, debilitating, draining emotions that were overwhelming him into positive, productive emotions and behavior.

Shortly after I received his email, we talked. He told me the work he had completed was for the senior leadership team. He noted that if he had not used the techniques, it would have taken him two or three times as long to complete the work — and the result would not have been as good. His improvement is not uncommon.

As a side note, a retired vice president who reviewed the first draft of this book sent back his edits and suggestions. In the margin beside the quote above he wrote, "This happened in less than a week after the training? I don't think so!! I might believe a few months." My response was "Yes, it did! In less than a week!" That is the power available to people when they learn to manage their emotions!

Change Effectiveness
When we examine the introduction and implementation of change on individuals and on organizations, it's not unusual to find that change is not only resisted, but also actually avoided.

Figure 7.
The Emotional Roller Coaster Ride that Occurs When a Change is Announced

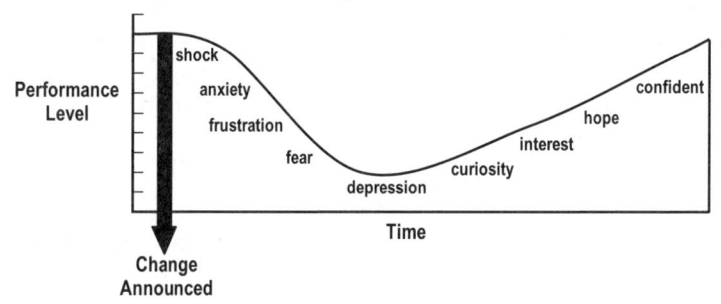

When a change is announced there is a roller-coaster ride of emotions and these emotions diminish change effectiveness. As people experience these debilitating emotions, performance levels decline. Over time, as they learn more about the change or see that their negative assumptions about the change are not as bad as assumed, they may become cautiously curious, interested in the change, and even hopeful. But that typically takes several months to a year or two after the initial organizational introduction of the change.

Emotional Triggers
What causes us to experience negative emotions? The universal trigger of negative emotions is our perception of being threatened or endangered (Daniel Goleman, *Emotional Intelligence*). There are two major types of threats: physical and symbolic or psychological. While it's easy to identify physical threats, we actually experience symbolic threats more frequently.

Symbolic threats include:
- Threats to our security.
- Threats to our self-esteem.

- Threats to our dignity.
- Being treated unjustly.
- Being insulted or demeaned.
- Being frustrated in pursuing a goal important to us.

For example, what could occur at your work that would be a symbolic threat to your security? How about downsizing, or just the rumors about potential downsizing? One of the most interesting aspects of symbolic threats is that they are based on an individual's perception. For example, two people could be given the identical task or hear the same statement, and one may welcome the opportunity or information, while the other may perceive the assignment or statement as a threat. People frequently experience shock, anxiety, frustration, and fear as they consider the potential impact of a change on themselves and their families.

Real Change Today

Fifteen or twenty years ago when perhaps one change a year was introduced, management could wait for people to ride their emotional roller-coaster to see the positive side of change. Today's reality is change upon change upon change that occurs in rapid succession.

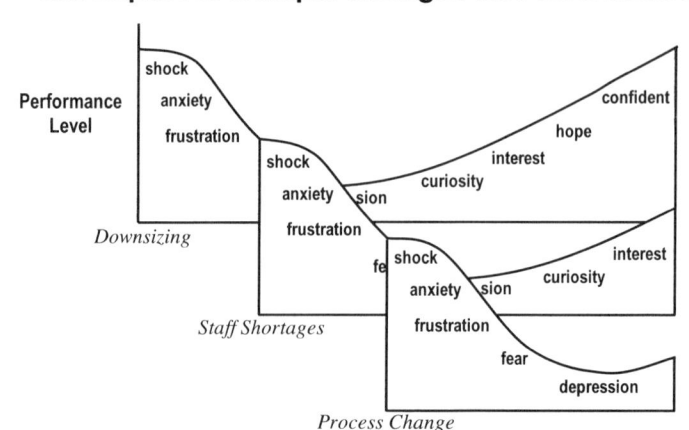

**Figure 8.
The Impact of Multiple Changes on Performance**

Performance Level

shock, anxiety, frustration — *Downsizing*

shock, anxiety, sion, frustration — *Staff Shortages*

fe, shock, anxiety, sion, frustration, fear, depression

curiosity, interest, hope, confident

curiosity, interest

Process Change

Without high levels of Emotional Intelligence skills, it's likely people and their performance will hinder an organizations ability to implement required changes efficiently or effectively. The result is that performance (productivity) will decrease and profits will lag.

Customer Service

As we move from the employee's portion into the customer's portion, we find emotions matter significantly here also. In his book, *Stress for Success,* James Loehr summarizes the impact of emotions on customers when he states, "Emotion drives everything. The most important component of customer service *is* emotion. Regardless of what we do to help a customer, how we make the customer *feel* emotionally is what counts."

Some companies are beginning to realize the importance of the *emotional* part of a customer's experience with a company's products, services, and people. In the *Fast Company* magazine article "Idea Fest" Marcus Buckingham is quoted, "Companies need to realize that, as economic beings, we behave emotionally most of the time. You can either build your business around that fact or risk losing your customers to somebody who understands and cares for them better." Some organizations are beginning to realize they need to create an emotional connection with their customers, whether it's on the phone or when the customer interacts with their product on the sales floor. Brand managers understand customers' emotions in making purchasing decisions and have integrated that understanding into marketing techniques. Some companies have even created executive positions that focus on creating a positive experience for their customers.

A good example comes from a story a colleague told:

> Jennifer, one of our senior associates, usually wears bright beautiful clothing when she and I are co-facilitating the development program. One day, I remarked about her colorful outfit. I asked where she bought it, assuming she would say somewhere in the Chicago area, which is near her home. She said she bought it in a shop in a small town about an hour and a half south of Chicago, so I asked her why she shopped there.
>
> She told me the first time she went into the store, she was greeted by a clerk who introduced herself, asked Jennifer's name, and told Jennifer she would be available to help whenever needed. Jennifer selected several items to try on and took them to the dressing room. As she tried on outfits, she hung those that didn't fit over the dressing room door. As she did, the clerk was there to help and would ask, "Would you like me to get you a different size or color?" She also offered her honest opinion about how the outfits complemented or detracted from Jennifer's coloring, height, and body shape.

Questions and honest, authentic answers such as these enabled the clerk to help Jennifer in her decision process and reinforced her self-esteem. The support the clerk provided also enabled Jennifer to *feel* good about herself, and confident about her purchase. Customer service is all about paying attention to how the customer *feels* so the customer is pleased (emotionally positive) with the experience.

Sample Results

As you've read the previous parts of this chapter, you have gained a good understanding of what Emotional Intelligence is and the competencies that comprise Emotional Intelligence. You have seen the impact both well-managed and mismanaged emotions can have on leadership abilities, performance, stress, health, and resiliency to change. Following is a small sample of some of the results achieved by groups of clients in our development programs by applying the techniques taught in Chapter 3.

Two to three months after attending our programs participants are interviewed and asked if they have experienced any improvement in the Personal Goals they selected before attending the program. If so, they are asked to provide an estimated percentage improvement.

The nine intrapersonal topics in the figure below represent goals that can be achieved by using the techniques. This data was collected two months after the program and represents the average improvement noted by the participants.

Figure 9.
Average Estimated Improvements Achieved by Executives in Intrapersonal Areas

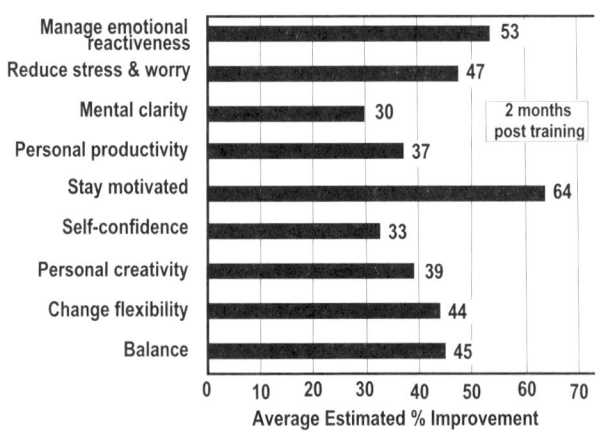

Intrapersonal Area	Average Estimated % Improvement (2 months post training)
Manage emotional reactiveness	53
Reduce stress & worry	47
Mental clarity	30
Personal productivity	37
Stay motivated	64
Self-confidence	33
Personal creativity	39
Change flexibility	44
Balance	45

Source: Byron Stock & Associates

The data shown below is typical of results achieved in interpersonal skills by executives, managers, and individuals at a variety of levels two to three months after training.

Figure 10.
Average Estimate of Improvement Reported by Executives in Interpersonal Areas

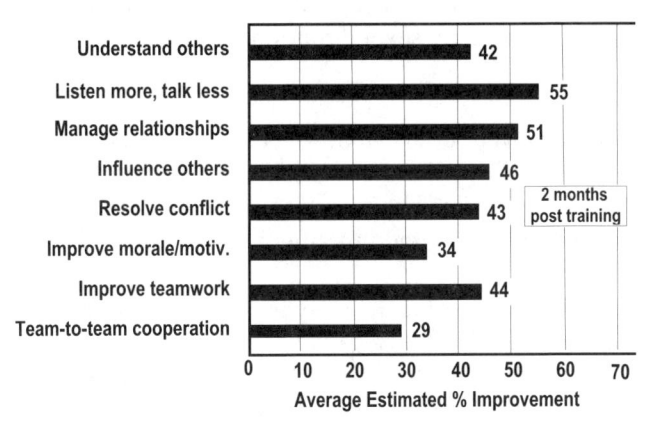

Area	Average Estimated % Improvement (2 months post training)
Understand others	42
Listen more, talk less	55
Manage relationships	51
Influence others	46
Resolve conflict	43
Improve morale/motiv.	34
Improve teamwork	44
Team-to-team cooperation	29

Source: Byron Stock & Associates

Too Good to be True?

I know what you're thinking — "This looks too good to be true!" That's almost exactly what one executive told us two months after attending our applied Emotional Intelligence skill-building program. During his Impact Interview he said, "When we began this program some people said, 'This can't work. It looks too good to be true. Even a 5% improvement would be impossible.' But I've seen 40-50% improvements in my three personal goal areas. I now have tools to make choices about how I feel, how I react. These techniques do work if you use them."

How could this be? The improvements participants report to us indicate just how detrimental mismanaged emotions can be and how much of our time is taken up by worry, frustration, second-guessing ourselves, conflict, ruminating on past events and conversations. Since our emotions impact so many aspects of our lives, when we learn to recognize and manage them more effectively, several areas of our work and family lives improve.

How Much Would It Take?

If you are still a little skeptical of the improvement numbers reported by participants, take a conservative approach. Would you be satisfied if you could achieve just half of those improvements? The point is, this data represents the improvement people in organizations are actually experiencing as a result of practicing and applying these techniques. And you can, too!

Following the development programs, participants are asked to share examples of their experiences. A Director of Engineering Services with a high-tech company responded with this story:

> A customer with an existing multi-million dollar contract requested the contract be reduced by several million dollars.
>
> The director was on a plane flying to South America for the meeting when he became aware of his anxiety about it. He used one of the techniques he had learned to transform his anxiety into more positive, productive feelings and behavior, and then used another technique to generate creative ideas around this situation.
>
> He went into the meeting the next day feeling positive. He was able, in-the-moment, to handle the negative emotions he felt when an engineer kept "picking at" his ideas. He walked out of the meeting with an *increase* in contract price (to the tune of several million dollars) instead of a decrease!

Additional Results

There are a number of additional examples of results that have been achieved by people who learn and use the techniques. See Chapter 4 for illustrative stories, client comments, and more results data.

Section III
THE SCIENCE OF EMOTIONAL INTELLIGENCE

This section includes a summary of much of the research presented in the Institute of HeartMath's *Research Overview*, 1997. In this Overview HeartMath presents their research and others' demonstrating that the heart communicates with the brain through several pathways, and, thus profoundly influences brain function.

Your Brain: Three In One — Which One Do You Use?

You've probably heard of the left and right side of the brain. One new way scientists examine the brain today is to look at it from an evolutionary point-of-view. In so doing, they focus on three brains; the first or lower-level, the second or mid-level, and the third or higher-level brain.

The first or lower-level brain (see Figure 11) is composed of the brain stem and the cerebellum. It's also known as the "reptilian brain" because reptiles have this kind of brain. Its main control is reflex and instinct. This brain doesn't really "think." Its basic function is daily control of bodily systems. For example, this is the brain that puts the right enzymes in your stomach to digest food so you don't have to think consciously about it.

Figure 11.
A Simplified Representation of the First or Lower-Level Brain

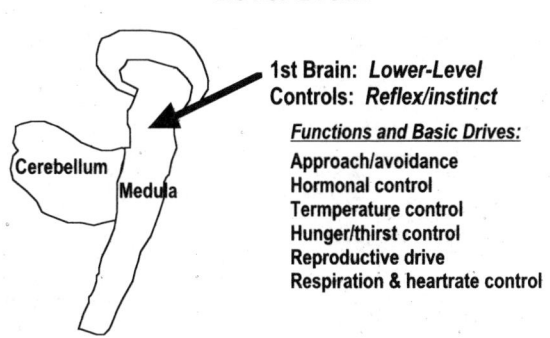

Cerebellum
Medula

1st Brain: *Lower-Level*
Controls: *Reflex/instinct*

<u>Functions and Basic Drives:</u>
Approach/avoidance
Hormonal control
Termperature control
Hunger/thirst control
Reproductive drive
Respiration & heartrate control

The second brain (see Figure 12) is referred to as the mid-level brain, because of its position between the lower and higher functioning brain. It has the capacity for hindsight. For example, if we ate some wild berries while we were in the woods and they upset our stomach, this brain would remind us not to eat them again. Its basic functions and drives have to do with emotion.

Figure 12.
The Second or Mid-Level Brain Is Also Known as The Limbic Center or the Emotional Brain

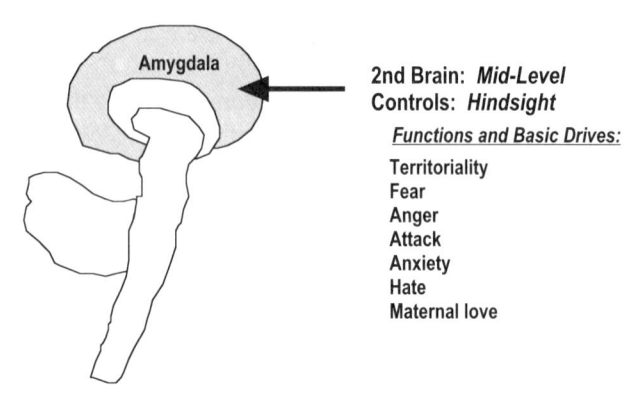

2nd Brain: *Mid-Level*
Controls: *Hindsight*

Functions and Basic Drives:

Territoriality
Fear
Anger
Attack
Anxiety
Hate
Maternal love

It doesn't think (reason) per se, but it will warn us of danger and act very quickly to keep us out of threatening situations. This is the area of the brain we associate with "fight or flight" reactions.

The third or higher-level brain has the capacity for foresight. It can look into the future and answer the question, "What if?" This brain has the capacity for differentiation of thoughts and emotions. It can discriminate between appropriate and inappropriate behaviors. This is the brain that solves problems. You were hired for your use of this brain!

Figure 13.
The Third or Higher-Level Brain Is Known as the Thinking Brain or Neocortex

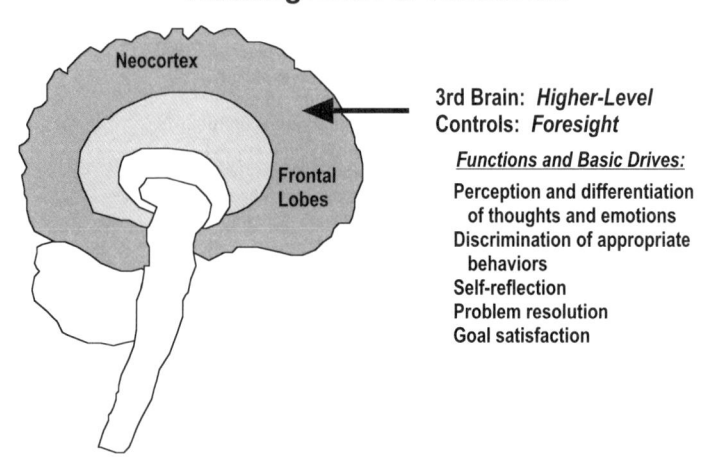

3rd Brain: *Higher-Level*
Controls: *Foresight*

Functions and Basic Drives:

Perception and differentiation of thoughts and emotions
Discrimination of appropriate behaviors
Self-reflection
Problem resolution
Goal satisfaction

Negative Emotions Inhibit Brain Function

Information comes into our second brain (Emotional Brain or Limbic System) through our eyes and our ears. In the Limbic System is a component of the brain known as the amygdala, which acts as a security guard. It monitors the information coming from our eyes and our ears. Its job is to protect us from threats, whether they're physical threats or symbolic (psychological) threats.

If the amygdala perceives something as a threat, it triggers our Autonomic Nervous System (ANS) to take action immediately, before the information can make its way up to our third (Thinking) brain. So, negative emotions keep us from using our third brain effectively. Instead, when we are upset we get a second-brain reaction, "fight" or "flight." The old saying, "I was so upset I couldn't think straight!" is, physiologically, absolutely accurate and true. Sometimes when this is happening, we say things without really thinking about them. In the extreme, when a person is not in rational control of himself, we might say he is "acting like a madman."

**Figure 14.
Negative Emotions Inhibit Our Ability to Think Clearly**

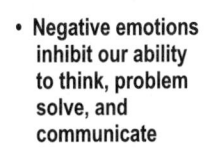

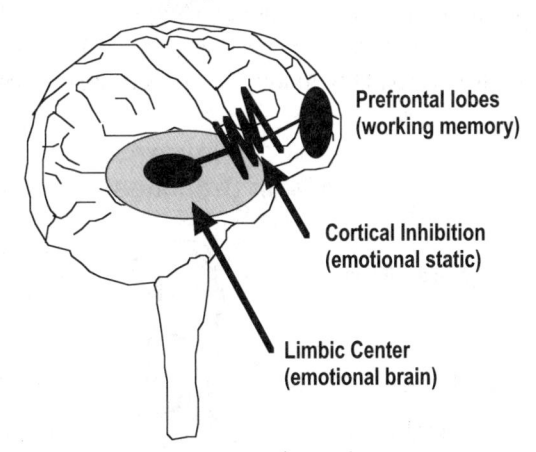

- Negative emotions inhibit our ability to think, problem solve, and communicate

- It occurs whether we are aware of it or not

Prefrontal lobes (working memory)

Cortical Inhibition (emotional static)

Limbic Center (emotional brain)

Physical Activities and Coordination

When we experience negative emotions, whether we're aware of it or not, we don't think clearly. Negative emotions also disrupt control of our physical actions. Have you ever gotten mad at yourself while playing sports? What happens to your performance? It decreases, right? This is an example of how negative emotions hamper your physical performance.

Emotional Memory

Our emotional memories also act to protect us from threats, whether current or past, perceived or real. In this case, when there is incoming information through our eyes or through our ears, our amygdala checks its memory bank to see how closely this information matches past physical or symbolic threats. If our amygdala finds a threatening memory that is similar to current incoming information, it causes us to act without thinking. So, before we know it, or consciously think about it, our Autonomic Nervous System is activated and we experience either a "fight" or "flight" reaction.

For example, if we are given an assignment or a project that is similar to one we worked on in the past that was difficult or caused us problems, we may be anxious about the project. This happens before the information can get up to our thinking brain where we can reason and think about the situation. We may avoid it (flight) or actively try to shove it off (fight) onto someone else. Current events that look like events from our past may trigger an emotional hijacking. We can end up reacting to things rather than thinking clearly about them in the "here and now."

Your Autonomic Nervous System

Your Autonomic Nervous System (ANS) is composed of two main pathways. The sympathetic pathway speeds things up — like the gas pedal in a car — while the parasympathetic pathway slows things down like the brake pedal.

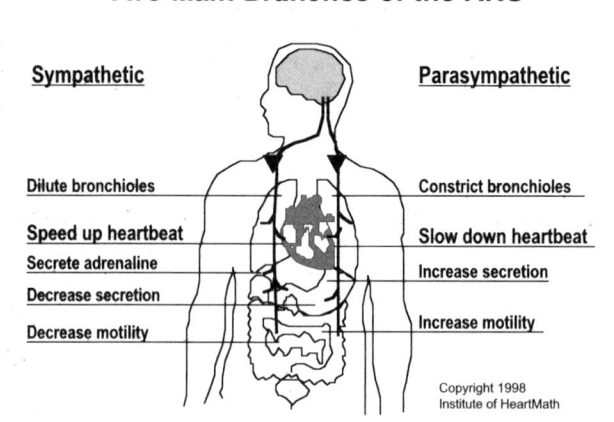

**Figure 15.
Two Main Branches of the ANS**

Sympathetic
- Dilute bronchioles
- Speed up heartbeat
- Secrete adrenaline
- Decrease secretion
- Decrease motility

Parasympathetic
- Constrict bronchioles
- Slow down heartbeat
- Increase secretion
- Increase motility

Copyright 1998
Institute of HeartMath

All ANS signals originate in our brain and are sent to our various organs and subsystems as indicated by the lines and arrowheads. Our heart, brain, immune, hormonal, respiratory, and digestive systems are all connected by this network of nerves.

Your Nervous System in Balance

The most efficient and effective way for our nervous system to work is in balance, that is, when the system is speeding up and slowing down rhythmically. If we continue with the car analogy, it's like having a one-footed driver–with one foot on either the gas or on the brake. A one-footed driver can make smooth transitions between the brake and the gas pedal.

"Dis-Ease" and Our Autonomic Nervous System

Our Autonomic Nervous System regulates many of our body's functions automatically. Imbalance in our ANS occurs when negative emotions are being experienced, causing both the sympathetic and parasympathetic to be activated. It's like having a two-footed driver with one foot on the gas and the other on the brake, sometimes pressing on both at the same time or almost the same time. Many disease states are correlated with imbalances in our nervous system, including:

- Anxiety
- Asthma
- Fatigue
- Depression
- Dizziness
- Fibromyalgia
- Arrhythmia
- Hypertension
- Hypoglycemia
- Irritable bowel
- Migraines
- Chemical sensitivity
- Mitral valve prolapse
- Nausea
- Panic disorder
- Premenstrual syndrome
- Sleep disorder

Source: Institute of HeartMath

Are you, your colleagues, or family members experiencing any of the above? The point is your body is in "dis-ease" when you have a lack of balance in your nervous system. Negative emotions contribute to "dis-ease" throughout your body.

Your Immune System

Immunoglobulin A (IgA) is found in our saliva and throughout our digestive tract. It's our first line of immune system defense against viruses. The higher the level of IgA in our body, the better. The Institute of HeartMath designed and conducted a clinical study to examine the impact of emotion on immune system levels, specifically IgA.

Figure 16.
Emotions Can Impact Your Immune System Function Dramatically

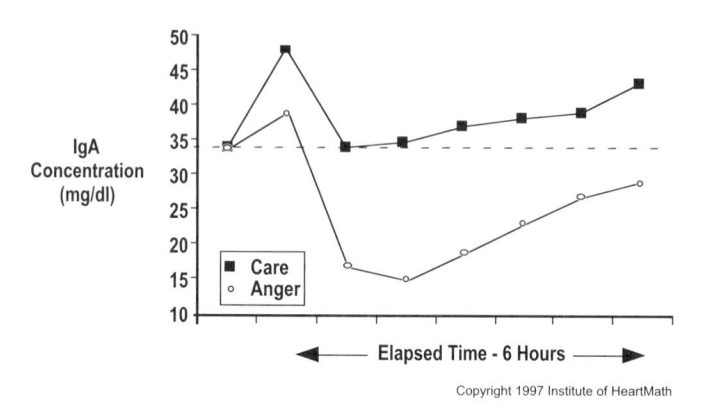

IgA Concentration (mg/dl)

■ Care
○ Anger

◄——— Elapsed Time - 6 Hours ———►

Copyright 1997 Institute of HeartMath

At the beginning of the clinical study, a saliva sample was taken from volunteers. The average starting level was about 34 milligrams per deciliter. Participants were then asked to recall for five minutes something that made them angry. Another saliva sample was taken at the end of the five minutes and the reading went up to about 39 (see the line with circles). That's good — the higher the IgA level the better.

But look at what happened over the next six hours. The IgA level fell dramatically and when it came back up, it didn't come back up to the starting value. The conclusion is that five minutes of recalled anger can depress this essential part of our immune system for up to six hours.

For example, you're driving to work on the expressway when some "idiot" squeezes in between your car and the one in front of you. Anger and rage rise up in you. You can't believe that someone would be that stupid. He pulls over into the fast lane and speeds ahead. How could someone be so inconsiderate and dangerous? You look ahead to see if you can see his license plate so you can report him to the police. You're fuming and you relive his pulling that stupid stunt a couple of more times in your mind before you get to work.

What have you just done to your immune system for the rest of the day? What have you done to your mental clarity? How is that likely to impact the rest of your day?

Now the good news — this time the volunteers were asked to recall for five minutes something or someone they sincerely cared for. Another saliva sample was taken after the five minutes. IgA had risen to about 50 (see the line with squares). Look at what happened over the next six hours. The IgA level did fall, but only back to the starting value. Then over the next six hours it rose. The conclusion is, recalling positive emotions can boost an important component of our immune system health.

The Perception Cycle

Perception is a process of acquiring and interpreting information from our senses. It is not a process of fact but of *interpretation* — a process of choosing a way to look at an event.

Figure 17.
How Perception Triggers a Series of Effects

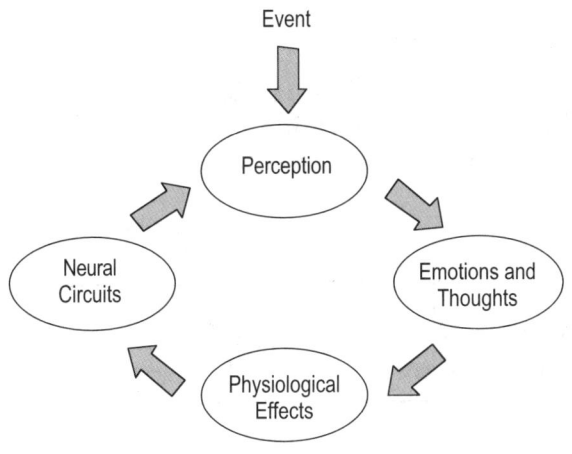

Event → Perception → Emotions and Thoughts → Physiological Effects → Neural Circuits → Perception

Copyright 1996 Institute of HeartMath

Typically, an event occurs (we hear someone say something or we see something). We then choose a way of interpreting the event, a perception of the event. For example, we may choose to interpret an assignment our boss gives us as difficult and of no value to the organization. Our choosing of that perception then affects our emotions and our thoughts.

Emotions we experience may include frustration, fear, resentment or panic. And the thoughts might include some unpleasant things about the boss, how overworked we are, or how many days we will have to work late. Those emotions and thoughts lead to a myriad of physiological effects. For example, Hafen et al. note in *The Health Effects of Attitudes, Emotions and Relationships* that feeling stressful emotions cause 1,400 different biochemical changes in the body. If the emotions are negative and persist for a while, they can lower immune system function and cause excess Cortisol (known as the stress hormone) to be produced in our bodies. Those physiological changes impact the neural circuits in our brain to reinforce the perception we chose in the first place.

One of the best ways to create a change in the perception cycle is to become aware of the events or "triggers" that lead to unproductive perceptions, negative emotions and thoughts, and harmful physiological consequences to our bodies.

Emotions Affect Heart Rhythms

Your pulse rate, or "resting heart rate," is actually an average because your heart is speeding up and slowing down all the time. The beat-to-beat change in your heart's rate is called heart rate variability (HRV). It reflects the activation of the sympathetic and parasympathetic parts of your Autonomic Nervous System.

Figure 18.
The Emotion of Frustration Negatively Affects the Heart Rate Variability Pattern

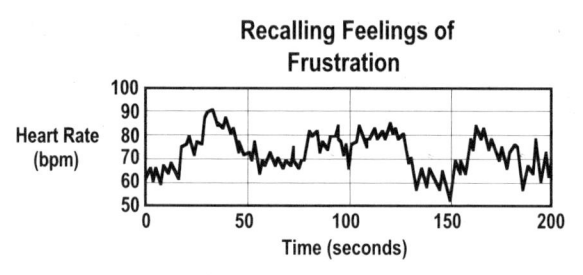

Recalling Feelings of Frustration

Copyright 1996 Institute of HeartMath

Notice in the figure the heart rhythm is very chaotic; it speeds up and slows down haphazardly. It's not smooth and rhythmic. In fact, this chaotic form is actually a mapping of the person's Autonomic Nervous System. When the line is going up, the sympathetic part of the system is engaged, speeding things up. Whenever the line is going down, the parasympathetic part of the system is activated, slowing the heart rate down. In the figure, you'll notice how quickly the line changes from up to down and vice versa.

This speeding up and slowing down is like that driver with one foot on the gas pedal and the other on the brake. The car lurches back and forth, the brake lights flash off and on, and the occupants get jostled around. This is hard on the brakes, shocks, engine, and drive train.

Research at the Institute of HeartMath has confirmed that whenever we're experiencing negative emotions, it's not only hard on our heart, but on other systems in our body as well. This incoherent, chaotic pattern created by frustration (or other negative emotions) leads to what scientists call cortical inhibition, limiting our ability to access what's in the neocortex, our "thinking" brain.

Emotional/Cortical Facilitation

The good news is that positive emotions facilitate your ability to think, problem solve, and communicate. Unlike emotional hijacking, which is caused by negative emotions, positive emotions facilitate the link between your emotional brain (limbic system) and your thinking brain (neocortex). Experiencing positive emotions enables you to think quickly and clearly. This is a profound statement, especially when you consider how much negativity and anxiety exist in most organizations today.

Impact of Positive Emotions on Brain Function

Positive emotions act like a lubricant between the emotional brain and the thinking brain. Positive emotions enable us to make faster, better decisions, seeing all the possibilities before us.

Have you ever gotten into a heated discussion and found that you couldn't think of the words you needed to say? That is emotional hijacking. Then, two hours later, after the negative emotions have had time to clear out on their own you get the "Aha!" But why wait two hours? Transforming to positive emotions enables you to get the "Aha!" *in-the-moment*! This saves a lot of energy.

Figure 19.
How Positive Emotions Facilitate Access to Your Thinking Brain

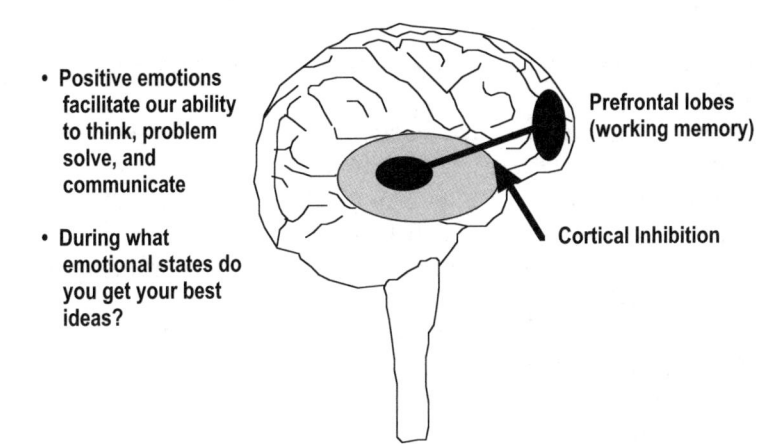

- Positive emotions facilitate our ability to think, problem solve, and communicate

- During what emotional states do you get your best ideas?

Prefrontal lobes (working memory)

Cortical Inhibition

Heart-To-Brain Communication

You've learned that the Autonomic Nervous System signals originate in the brain and are sent to all your organs and subsystems, including your heart. The heart communicates with the brain via two primary pathways, the vagus nerve and the sympathetic afferent nerves in the spinal column.

**Figure 20.
Neurological Pathways Through Which the Heart Communicates with the Brain**

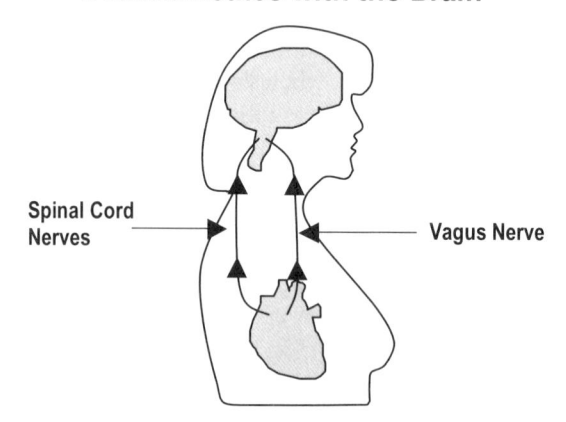

So, between your Autonomic Nervous System (from brain to heart) and your vagus nerve and spinal cord nerves (from heart to brain), there is a two-way flow of information. The key point is your heart influences your brain, and what occurs in your heart affects your thinking and your performance — instantaneously.

The Power of Your Heart

Most of us believe that our brain controls our entire body. When we examine new research, we find, in fact, the heart plays a significant role in this two-way communication system and in how well our brain processes information. For example:

- The heart starts beating in the fetus before the brain has developed.
- The source of the heartbeat is within the heart.
- When the heart starts beating in the womb (about seven days after conception), it causes all of the other fetal cells to differentiate — that is, they start transforming into specific cells such as liver cells, stomach cells, bone cells, blood cells, etc.
- The heart has its own "brain." It has 40,000 neurons (or brain cells) embedded in it. This operates as its own intrinsic nervous system.
- Our heart communicates with our brain in four ways (neurologically via neurological impulses, biochemically via hormones, biophysically via

pressure waves, and energetically via the electromagnetic field it generates with each beat).
- With every beat, our heart produces an electromagnetic field 5,000 times stronger than the field produced by our brain.
- With every beat, our heart generates 40-60 times more electrical amplitude than our brain.
- The signal from our heart can be measured anywhere on our body. It permeates every cell.
- If you're put in a room lined with electromagnetic sensors on the walls, the electromagnetic signals from your heart can be detected eight feet away from your body.

Source: The Institute of HeartMath

As you can see, our heart is more than a pump. It communicates information to our body and brain through a variety of methods and pathways.

Coherent Heart Rhythms

Notice how smooth and coherent this heart rhythm is. Instead of a "two footed driver," we have a "one-footed driver."

Figure 21.
The Emotion of Appreciation Positively Affects the Heart's Rhythm

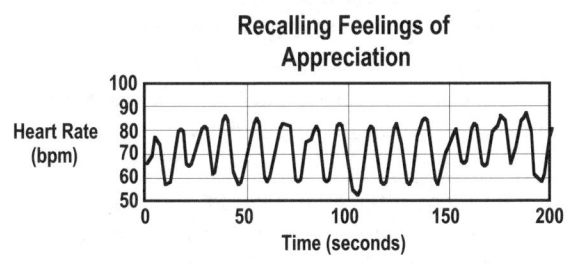

Recalling Feelings of Appreciation

Heart Rate (bpm)

Time (seconds)

Copyright 1996 Institute of HeartMath

The foot is either on the gas (going faster), or on the brake (going slower). This smooth, rhythmic pattern created by recalling positive emotions (such as appreciation) leads to cortical facilitation. When we're feeling positive emotions, we get our best ideas.

Where are you and what are you doing when you get your best ideas? More importantly, what are you *feeling* when you get your best ideas? Perhaps you get your best ideas in the shower. Or perhaps you get your best ideas after a good night's sleep. Conversely, most of us do *not* get our most creative ideas when we are anxious, worried, or frustrated. Sure, we all can think of situations where we came up with a creative idea during a highly stressful situation, but this is clearly the exception, not the rule. Moreover, being stuck in negative emotions is not sustainable in the long-term as a method of generating breakthrough ideas and solutions.

The point is, positive emotions enable us to think broadly and quickly, with full access to all we know. And the coherent, rhythmic signals coming from the heart to the brain facilitate that process.

Coherence and Biological Oscillators
In the various systems in our bodies we have pacemaker cells. They are in our heart, respiratory system, digestive system, hormonal system, etc. These are referred to as biological oscillators. These pacemaker cells cause the systems to oscillate or operate at a rhythm, pace, or rate. Research on these biological systems shows that less powerful biological oscillators will "entrain," or get "in sync," with the strongest, dominant one within the body. This state of synchronization among pacemaker cells in various biological systems represents a highly efficient mode of bodily function.

Entrainment and Our Body's Biological Oscillators
Since our heart is the dominant "oscillator" in our body, all of the other pacemaker cells within different systems try to match-up or to get "in sync" with the rhythm generated by our heart. When we're feeling negative emotions (which cause our heart to beat chaotically), the various pacemaker cells cannot get "in sync" and therefore do not operate efficiently. On the other hand, when we're feeling positive emotions (which cause our heart to beat smoothly and rhythmically), all of our biological systems will easily get "in sync" and work more efficiently and effectively.

The emotions we experience have an impact on the efficiency and effectiveness of our heart and biological systems in our body. Negative emotions, over time, can lead to "dis-ease" in some of these systems, including our heart. Positive emotions enable the systems in our body to work efficiently. In fact, positive emotions enable the systems in our body to work so efficiently our brain and heart can literally be on the same wavelength.

Head/Heart Entrainment
On the following page the top left graph shows a very smooth, coherent heart rate pattern. To the right of that is a graph of the frequency distribution of those heart beats. Because our heart produces electromagnetic energy, the frequencies of that energy can be measured. Notice there is a peak frequency at about 0.1 Hz. (see arrow). The bottom left graph shows actual brainwave data of the same person at the same time. To the right of that is a graph of the

frequency distribution of those brain waves. Notice there is a peak at about 0.1 Hz. (see bottom arrow).

Figure 22.
Frequency Analysis Shows Entrainment of Heart and Brain When a Person Feels Appreciation

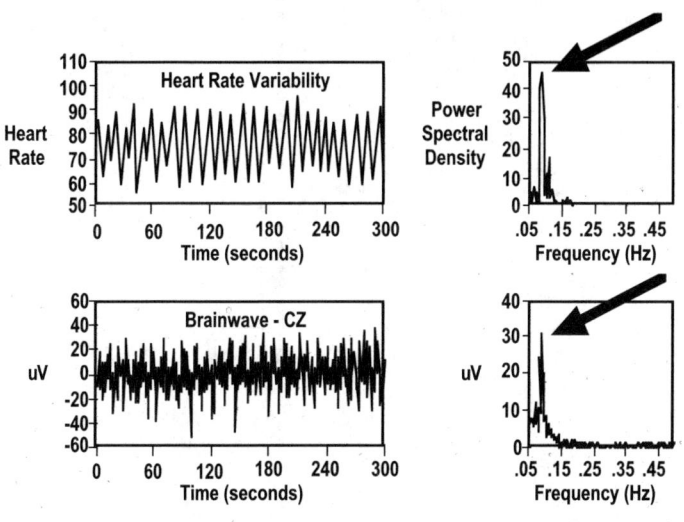

Copyright 1996 Institute of HeartMath

The two graphs at the right show when a person is feeling sincere appreciation, his/her heart and brain are literally on the same frequency. They're "in sync." There is an efficient and effective transfer of information between them. You can create this coherent, efficient communication using the techniques in the book.

Creating Inner Coherence

Notice the left portion of the graphs on the following page. The three measures are not coherent or "in sync." The black line in Figure 23 represents the point at which the person started using the "Freeze-Frame" technique (one of the techniques you'll master in Chapter 3). The Freeze-Frame technique enabled the person to quickly transform his emotions into positive, productive emotions. Notice how little time it took to get these three systems "in sync."

**Figure 23.
Three Different Biological Systems Come into
Coherence with the Freeze-Frame Technique**

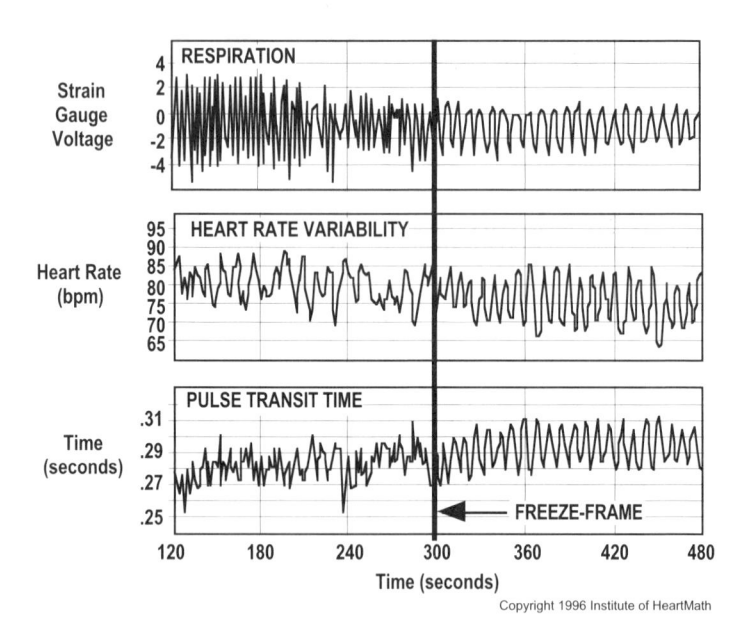

Copyright 1996 Institute of HeartMath

How Our Brain Learns

When a child is born, s/he has all the neurons (brain cells) s/he will ever have. The way s/he learns to do anything — walk, open a door, drive a car — is through a process where axons and dendrites (parts of the neuron) connect thousands of neurons together in a pathway (see Figure 24).

Just as physical movements such as walking, driving, opening a door, turning on a light switch, crossing our legs, eating with a fork, etc., become "stereotyped" and automatic through repetition, so do mental and emotional responses and attitudes. As we learn, neurons connect to each other in a web or network to process information or store memories, abilities, physical coordination, ongoing attitudes, etc. The branching and thickening of the dendrites and connections to other neurons increase, correlating to the amount of experience and learning. The more we repeat an activity, like walking, the more connected these thousands of neurons become and the less conscious thought or energy we have to expend to do the activity. After practicing for a while, the activity becomes very easy to do and requires almost no thought.

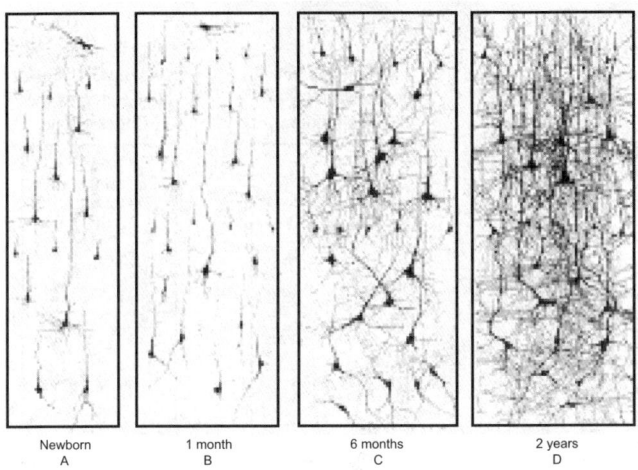

Figure 24.
Change in Brain Cell Connectivity from Newborn to 24 Months

| Newborn | 1 month | 6 months | 2 years |
| A | B | C | D |

Reprinted by permission of the publisher from THE POSTNATAL DEVELOPMENT OF THE HUMAN CEREBRAL CORTEX, VOLS. I-VIII by Jesse LeRoy Conel, Cambridge, Mass.: Harvard University Press, Copyright © 1939, 1975 by the President and Fellows of Harvard College.

As long as we choose to keep doing it that way, this learned pathway of connected neurons will stay intact.

Choosing a New Way of Responding

If we choose to do an activity or respond to a situation in a new way, a better way, we can create new pathways that serve us better. Figure 25 on the following page illustrates this. Over time, the more we practice the new way, the easier it becomes, as emphasized by the thicker weight of the line in the right frame. On the other hand, with less and less use, the old pathway will lose its connectivity (thinner line in the middle frame).

The more you practice using the techniques in this book, the easier and faster they will become. Using them frequently will provide you with a *chosen* way of responding to what had been emotionally difficult situations. After practicing these techniques for a few weeks, they will become so easy to do they will require almost no thought or conscious energy or effort on your part.

**Figure 25.
Replacing Old Ways with a New Learned Way of Responding**

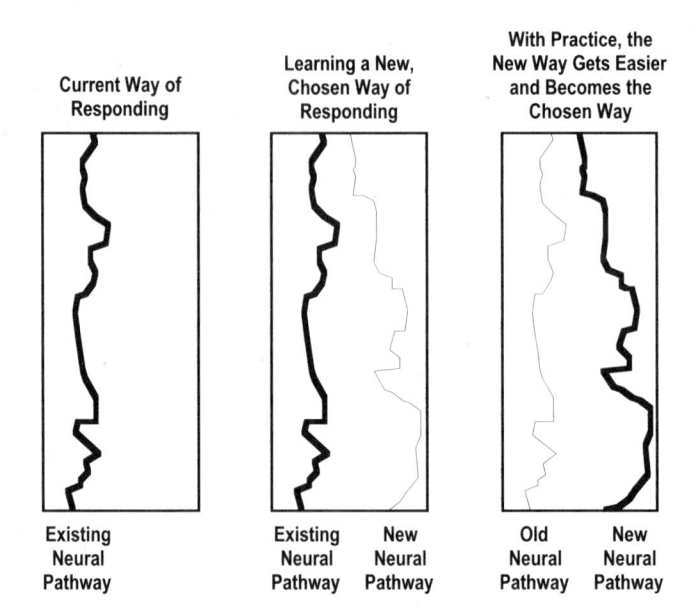

Current Way of Responding	Learning a New, Chosen Way of Responding	With Practice, the New Way Gets Easier and Becomes the Chosen Way
Existing Neural Pathway	Existing Neural Pathway / New Neural Pathway	Old Neural Pathway / New Neural Pathway

Summary

Emotional Intelligence skills, both intrapersonal and interpersonal, are learnable. Unlike IQ, we can get better at managing and using our emotions to help ourselves and improve our relationships. Learning how to engage and use positive emotions can improve the quality of our thinking, communicating, and health. With practice, we can learn new ways to manage, control, and use our emotions to be more effective at work and at home. Physiological research into how our brain, heart, and other biological systems are affected by emotions provides conclusive evidence that negative emotions hamper our thinking and our health and that positive emotions facilitate them.

Key Points
- The purpose of developing our Emotional Intelligence is to help us make better decisions about what to say or do next (or *not* say or do).
- Emotional Intelligence is a different way of being smart.
- As an ingredient of excellent performance, Emotional Intelligence is twice as important as technical skills and IQ combined.
- Stress is the result of negative emotions and beliefs that occur whenever people are unable to cope with the demands from their environment.
- The universal trigger of negative emotions is the perception of being threatened.

- Negative emotions contribute to "dis-ease."
- Our heart is a powerful source of energy, information, and impact on our thinking and our body's systems.
- By managing our emotions we can keep ourselves at peak performance and health.
- Stress is an internal reaction — a perception — to an event.

CHAPTER 2

PREPARATION

WHAT WILL MAKE YOU SUCCESSFUL?

What will make you successful in improving your emotional competence? There's a very simple answer to that question — personal motivation, remembering, practicing use of the techniques, and reflection.

Personal Motivation

Your motivation to use the techniques in this book begins by determining what you want to improve and what isn't working well for you. The Personal Goal-Setting section in this chapter will help you do that. Another source of personal motivation is to read about people like you who have benefited by using the techniques. To do this, there are four areas in the book to choose from. All of them can be found in Chapter 4. They include...
1. Illustrative stories from clients describing how they have benefited by using the techniques in various situations.
2. Client's comments about each of the techniques.
3. Client's comments about each of the Personal Goals.
4. Measured results data from groups of people in companies and government agencies who have learned the techniques in our applied Emotional Intelligence skill-building development programs.

Remembering

Remembering to use the techniques is important, but it is not hard. The positive effects you experience from using the techniques will be a motivator in helping you continue to use them. Here are five things you can do to help you remember to use the techniques:
1. In your day planner, PDA, or personal notebook you use to keep track of your calendar, simply write the name or initials of the techniques everyday for a month. Or put in a daily reminder in your calendar in your computer that pops up throughout the day to remind you to use the techniques.
2. From our website (http://www.ByronStock.com/resources.html) download an electronic file to create reminder stickers. Put stickers in appropriate places both at work and home.
3. Receive free weekly email reminders. They contain reminders about using the techniques and positive inspirational quotes. Go to our website at http://www.ByronStock.com/resources.html to sign-up for them.

4. Peer coaching has been shown to be one of the most powerful factors in determining whether or not an individual will remember and use a new technique/skill. A simple Peer Coaching process and sample materials are provided in this chapter.
5. This book itself is a great visual reminder. Carry it with you or keep it on your desk.

Use of the Techniques

There are practice pages, questions, and other materials to complete as you learn and use different techniques. Use them. This is an important part of learning and reinforcing. In Chapter 3, a section describing each technique gives you suggestions on when and where to use it both at work and outside of work.

The emotional self-awareness technique ("What Am I Feeling Right Now?") takes less than a few seconds to do. And the Freeze-Frame technique (the most valuable tool for most people) can, with practice, be done in a few seconds. Other techniques take a little more time. The point is investing a *little bit of time* will return huge benefits. Practicing each technique as recommended in each section is the fastest way to experience results.

Reflection

Finally, take a minute or two at the end of each day to reflect on how you're improving. Purposefully notice your improvement. Notice the benefits you're receiving: *emotional benefits* (calmer, more peaceful, more patient, feeling hopeful); *physical benefits* (more energy, better sleep); *mental benefits* (more creative ideas, better focus); *relationship benefits* (less conflict, more help), and *performance benefits* (getting more done in less time, not procrastinating, influencing people).

The point is, by recognizing that you're making solid steady progress, you're likely to be persistent, and continue to be successful in achieving your Personal Goals.

SELECTING YOUR PERSONAL GOALS

What do you want to improve? In what ways do you want to change? Identifying your Personal Goals is the most important activity you need to do next. This will help motivate you and enable you to see how the techniques can improve your life. Put a checkmark by as many of the Personal Goals as you feel could be helpful to you, both professionally and personally.

Personal Goals

Intrapersonal Goals

Manage my emotional reactiveness (anger/discouragement) to people and situations — maintain better emotional balance.

Reduce stress and worry — decrease physical symptoms of stress such as sleeplessness, high blood pressure, indigestion, headaches — improve health.

Gain greater mental clarity — make better, faster decisions, trusting my intuition or "gut" to see solutions.

Increase personal productivity — manage priorities more efficiently and effectively — get more done in less time.

Stay motivated *in spite of* people or events — focus my energy on what I can influence or control, not on what's outside my control.

Develop more self-confidence — a greater belief in myself, my decisions, and in my own ability to interact with others — speak up with my ideas.

Increase personal creativity — identify more and different creative alternatives as actions or solutions to problems, projects, or assignments.

Increase change flexibility — be resilient in the face of change — think outside of my experience — develop a willingness to try new things.

Increase personal and professional balance — gain more enjoyment and quality out of life.

Interpersonal Goals

Understand others — the ability to understand a problem or situation from another's point-of-view.

Manage relationships more effectively — maintain respect and appreciation for others while identifying effective solutions to problems.

Listen more, talk less — inspire trust, build relationships.

Influence others — understand what's important to others and incorporate that information into my positioning of issues/initiatives.

Resolve/manage conflict — communicate more effectively in conflict situations — resolve differences constructively.

Improve morale/motivation — eliminate negativity and gossip and create a positive, open organizational climate of trust and acceptance.

Improve teamwork — cooperation, participation, trust, and full engagement in tasks to achieve goals.

Increase team-to-team cooperation/coordination — increase awareness of actions to successfully implement cross-boundary initiatives.

Adapted with permission, Shuman & Associates

As a guideline, at a minimum, select one or more Personal Goals from the intrapersonal goals. These are foundational and important to develop in order to experience improvement in any of the interpersonal goals.

My Top Three Personal Goals
Which three of the Personal Goals are most important for you at this time?

#1_____ #2_____ #3_____

Sample Goal and Situation Note Sheet
Review the Sample Goal and Situation Note Sheet on the following page. Use this sample as a guide when preparing your Goal and Situation Note Sheets.

First, choose one of your three Personal Goals from above and write it at the top of a Goal and Situation Note Sheet on the following pages (one goal per page). For your first goal, describe two or three situations occurring in your professional and/or personal life that caused you to select this goal. Think through these situations. Writing more, rather than less, will provide you with a greater awareness and insight into these situations and their impact on you. It will also make it easier for you to identify your triggers so that you can use the techniques to address the situations. Do the same for your second and third Personal Goals. This will take you about an hour to complete. Don't rush.

SAMPLE   Personal Goal and Situation Note Sheet

GOAL 1: Manage Emotional Reactiveness

Situation 1: Dick, he wastes my time, stupid requests, doesn't follow thru when he says he will do something   **How Often:** 8x/week

Effects (physical, mental, emotional, relationships, productivity) I get angry, make a bad impression, waste time, hard to focus immediately after

Desired State (what you would like things to be like) I'd be calmer, have a neutral impression of him, more productive   **Importance 1-5** 5

Situation 2: Volume of work overwhelms me

   How Often: 10x/week

Effects (physical, mental, emotional, relationships, productivity) Headaches, sore neck, sleeplessness, can't focus, waste time

Desired State (what you would like things to be like) Pick most important item and finish it, more productive and relaxed   **Importance 1-5** 5

Situation 3: Interruptions all day long

   How Often: 5-10x/day

Effects (physical, mental, emotional, relationships, productivity) Frustration, snippy with people, wastes my time, get mad and relive it at home

Desired State (what you would like things to be like) Handle it calmly, not raise my voice, get more done, be positive   **Importance 1-5** 5

Personal Goal and Situation Note Sheet

GOAL 1: _____

Situation 1: _____
_____ **How Often:** _____
Effects (physical, mental, emotional, relationships, productivity)_____
_____

Desired State (what you would like things to be like) _____
_____ **Importance 1-5** _____

Situation 2: _____
_____ **How Often:** _____
Effects (physical, mental, emotional, relationships, productivity)_____
_____

Desired State (what you would like things to be like) _____
_____ **Importance 1-5** _____

Situation 3: _____
_____ **How Often:** _____
Effects (physical, mental, emotional, relationships, productivity)_____
_____

Desired State (what you would like things to be like) _____
_____ **Importance 1-5** _____

Personal Goal and Situation Note Sheet

GOAL 2: _____

Situation 1: _____
_____ **How Often:** _____

Effects (physical, mental, emotional, relationships, productivity)_____
_____

Desired State (what you would like things to be like) _____
_____ **Importance 1-5** _____

Situation 2: _____
_____ **How Often:** _____

Effects (physical, mental, emotional, relationships, productivity)_____
_____

Desired State (what you would like things to be like) _____
_____ **Importance 1-5** _____

Situation 3: _____
_____ **How Often:** _____

Effects (physical, mental, emotional, relationships, productivity)_____
_____

Desired State (what you would like things to be like) _____
_____ **Importance 1-5** _____

Personal Goal and Situation Note Sheet

GOAL 3: _____

Situation 1: _____
_____ **How Often:** _____
Effects (physical, mental, emotional, relationships, productivity) _____
_____

Desired State (what you would like things to be like) _____
_____ **Importance 1-5** _____

Situation 2: _____
_____ **How Often:** _____
Effects (physical, mental, emotional, relationships, productivity) _____
_____

Desired State (what you would like things to be like) _____
_____ **Importance 1-5** _____

Situation 3: _____
_____ **How Often:** _____
Effects (physical, mental, emotional, relationships, productivity) _____
_____

Desired State (what you would like things to be like) _____
_____ **Importance 1-5** _____

CHAPTER 2 — PREPARATION 55

Identifying the Techniques for Your Personal Goals

For each Personal Goal, there are primary and secondary techniques that should be used to help attain it. "**P**" stands for a primary technique; "**s**" for a secondary technique. Circle your three Personal Goals and note the techniques you'll need to use regularly to experience improvement in reaching your goals.

Personal Goals and Techniques Matrix

PERSONAL GOALS \ TECHNIQUES	What Am I Feeling?	Freeze-Frame	Show Appreciation	Heart Lock-In	Intuitive Listening
Manage my emotional reactiveness	P	P		P	s
Reduce stress and worry	P	P		P	s
Gain greater mental clarity	P	P		P	s
Increase personal productivity	P	P	s	P	s
Stay motivated	P	P	s	P	s
Develop more self-confidence	P	P	s	P	s
Increase personal creativity		P		s	
Increase change flexibility	P	P		s	s
Increase personal/professional balance	P	P	s	P	s
Understand others	P	P	P		P
Listen more, talk less	P	P	P		P
Manage relationshhips more effectively	P	P	P	s	P
Influence others	P	P	P		P
Manage/resolve conflict	P	P	P		P
Improve morale/motivation	s	P	P	s	P
Improve teamwork	s	P	P	s	P
Improve team-to-team cooperation	s	P	P	s	P

PEER COACHING

Peer Coaching has been shown to be one of the most powerful factors in determining whether or not an individual will remember and use a new technique/skill. In a Peer Coaching arrangement, you develop a simple plan for the week and make a commitment to remember and practice one or more techniques as a means of achieving one of your Personal Goals. It's important that the plan is written down and the progress be noted, along with observations about what aided in developing the skill and what hindered.

Peer Coaching Note Sheet Sample and Blanks
On the following pages is a completed sample of a Peer Coaching Note Sheet. Review the sample to become familiar with the type of commitments you might possibly make to experience improvement and the type of notes you will keep to track your progress.

Timing
Initiate the Peer Coaching process after you have completed your Personal Goals and learned the first technique, "What Am I Feeling Right Now?"

Make Notes on Your First Peer Coaching Note Sheet
A blank version of the Peer Coaching Note Sheet can be found following the sample. Make as many copies of the blank Peer Coaching Note Sheet as you may need. Eight should be enough.

Next, Complete the Action Planning Portion of the Note Sheet
What Personal Goal do you want to improve? It's best to select one of the intrapersonal goals to begin with. Which of the techniques will you practice to achieve improvement? How often and when will you use the techniques? List those things that will help you remember to use the techniques.

Select a Peer Coach
Select a trusted and respected work colleague with whom you interact at least a few times a week. This person will be observing you to notice changes in the way you respond to situations that are typically difficult for you.

Review Your Peer Coaching Note Sheet with Your Peer Coach
Explain to your peer coach that you are learning and will be using some techniques to improve your Emotional Intelligence skills and that you would appreciate his/her help. Explain that his role is to…

- Meet with you once a week for about 15 minutes.
- Review and discuss your Action Plan for the week (which will be written on a Peer Coaching Note Sheet).
- Agree to observe your behavior throughout the week in the normal course of interacting with you and to notice (and keep notes of) any changes he sees, or any missed opportunities he sees.

At the next meeting a week later he is to...
- Listen as you share your successes, barriers you encountered, and lessons you learned for the week.
- Share his observations about your behavior and the improvements and difficulties he observed, and any missed opportunities.
- Offer ideas and suggestions to help you use the techniques as you plan for the coming week.

Commit to your Peer Coach that you really want his help. You will want to promise not to react negatively to constructive suggestions or his observations. Tell your peer coach that at this time you anticipate needing his help for about 6-8 weeks. You may choose to ask the coach to maintain confidentiality about the help he is providing you.

Keep Track of Your Progress for the Week
On the Tracking part of the Peer Coaching Note Sheet, jot down how you're progressing in using the techniques each day.

Use the Reflection portion daily at the end of the day or the beginning of the next day. Note your successes and reflect on them; this is an important part of self-motivation. Take a minute or two to recognize the progress you're making. Celebrate your accomplishments. In addition, jot down what helped you be successful. List any barriers that hampered your use of the techniques.

Before Meeting with Your Peer Coach
At the end of the week review your notes and decide if you are satisfied with your current level of improvement in your selected Personal Goal. If you are...
- Not satisfied, list ideas for continuing to improve and be prepared to solicit ideas from your peer coach.
- Satisfied, select a new Personal Goal and develop an Action Plan to achieve it.

Lastly, tentatively select a follow-up time and place for the next Peer Coaching discussion and be prepared to verify it with your coach.

SAMPLE Peer Coaching Note Sheet

Action Planning

I want to improve this Personal Goal: __Manage Emotional Reactiveness__

What techniques are you committing to use (and how often) to experience improvement in this Personal Goal?

WAIFRN — 5 times a day followed by Freeze-Frame

Freeze-Frame before each meeting

What support / reminders will help you use the techniques?

Put stickers in my day planner, on computer, in car

Tom — remind me whenever he sees me

Tracking

6-14 WAIFRN 5 times today and after negative emotions 4x

6-15 WAIFRN 4 times — Tom reminded me. Even did one when I was feeling positive. Used FF 4x before and 2x after. Before going in the house.

6-16 WAIFRN 4 times. FF after each meeting except one. Did FF after the meeting. Notice I'm feeling calmer going into meetings.

6-17 WAIFRN 5x. FF each time.

6-18 WAIFRN 5+ and getting much more aware throughout the day. FF are getting faster. Did one in meeting with Brian.

Weekend WAIFRN & FF because of the kids — I didn't yell at them!

SAMPLE　　　　**Peer Coaching Note Sheet**

Reflection

What were soome of the successes you had? _More relaxed in meeting with Bill. FF enables me to be more calm and speak up with ideas. Not upset with kids all weekend. Feeling more in control & not so stressed._

What did you do that enabled success? What facilitated your use of the techniques to achieve your goal? _Used the techniques! Having stickers around and actually stopping a few seconds to do the techniques. Knowing I was going to talk Tom about progress. Weekly reminders._

What were barriers? What got in the way of using the technqiues? _FF in a meeting on day 1 - couldn't remember the steps - easier day than usual. Thinking I don't have 1 minute to spare._

What did you learn about using the techniques during the past week? _Take the time to save time and my sanity. Stickers help. This is easier than I thought._

Are you satisfied with your current level of improvement in this Personal Goal?

　　　　Yes　　If yes, select a different Personal Goal to improve.
　　　　(No)　　If no, develop your Action Plan for next week.

What ideas do you and your peer coach have to use the techniques to experience more improvement in this Personal Goal? _Stick with the same plan. Tom will send me a humorous email reminder of encouragement. Have spouse remind me if I slip at home._

Next Peer Coaching Meeting

Date: _6-21_　　　Time: _11:30_　　　Location: _Conf. Room "B"_

Peer Coaching Note Sheet

Action Planning

I want to improve this Personal Goal: _____

What techniques are you committing to use (and how often) to experience improvement in this Personal Goal?

_____

_____

What support / reminders will help you use the techniques?

_____

_____

Tracking

_____

_____

_____

_____

_____

_____

_____

_____

_____

_____

_____

_____

_____

Peer Coaching Note Sheet

Reflection

What were soome of the successes you had? _____
_____
_____

What did you do that enabled success? What facilitated your use of the techniques to achieve your goal? _____
_____
_____

What were barriers? What got in the way of using the technqiues?
_____
_____

What did you learn about using the techniques during the past week?
_____
_____

Are you satisfied with your current level of improvement in this Personal Goal?

      Yes   If yes, select a different Personal Goal to improve.
      No   If no, develop your Action Plan for next week.

What ideas do you and your peer coach have to use the techniques to experience more improvement in this Personal Goal?
_____
_____

Next Peer Coaching Meeting

Date:_____ Time:_____ Location: _____

CHAPTER 3

SKILL-BUILDING TECHNIQUES

Congratulations! You are about to embark on an adventure of learning that has the potential to change the quality of your life. Here you will not just "learn about" the Emotional Intelligence techniques, you will have the opportunity to practice, to experience, to use the additional resources provided, and to profit from examples of others who have learned and used the techniques.

The five simple techniques that comprise the **SMART EMOTIONS** set of Emotional Skills are:
1. What Am I Feeling Right Now?
2. Freeze-Frame
3. Appreciation
4. Heart Lock-In
5. Intuitive Listening

TECHNIQUE #1 — WHAT AM I FEELING RIGHT NOW?

Completing This Section Enables You to...
- Enhance/expand your vocabulary of emotions.
- Recognize your own emotions and stressful feelings and events.
- Use the "What Am I Feeling Right Now?" (WAIFRN) technique.
- Identify people, events, and situations that trigger negative emotions in you.
- Quickly identify situations in which you want to change negative emotions into positive, productive emotions.
- Identify what's important in your life and the emotions those things release in you.

Overview
Emotional Self-Awareness, being aware of the emotions you are feeling, is *the* foundational skill needed to develop your Emotional Intelligence. Without it you have virtually no chance of regulating or choosing your emotions effectively. This section teaches you a simple technique to develop your awareness and broaden your emotional vocabulary.

When to Use the WAIFRN Technique

My workshops have helped me identify the following situations in which the "What Am I Feeling Right Now?" technique can be used. Look over each of the four lists that follow. You'll likely see situations similar to the ones bothering you. Use the "What Am I Feeling Right Now?" technique when…

Boss / Peers
- Boss blows up
- Boss jumps down my throat
- I'm being micromanaged
- Last minute requests
- Reorganization is announced
- I work with arrogant people
- I'm around executives
- Difficult meetings
- I see "politics"
- I receive advice about my career

Direct Reports
- Direct report makes a blunder
- Peppered with questions
- A project is completed
- I get interrupted
- Others don't meet expectations
- Discussing performance problems
- Supervisors misbehave
- Budget meeting

Personal
- My "hot button" is pushed
- Before/after a presentation
- I notice I'm talking louder
- When listening to voicemail
- Think about work at home
- My requests are turned down
- I procrastinate
- Around "egotists"
- While driving in traffic
- After a bad golf shot
- Airplane is delayed
- When reading email
- I bite my fingernails
- My neck muscles are sore
- In doctor's office
- During negative self-talk
- I feel my blood pressure rise
- Before answering phone at home

Family
- Kids make poor choices
- My child performs in a play
- Mother-in-law calls
- I visit mom in adult care home
- Talking about spouse's job
- Disciplining my child
- Children are sick
- Reviewing my child's grades
- Arguments at home
- On our family vacation
- My spouse thanks me
- Playing with grandchildren
- Baby formula on my suit
- Think about Mom's breast cancer
- Family conflict
- Discussing our day over dinner

Emotional Self-Awareness is Fundamental
In research conducted by Richard Boyatzis and Michelle Burckle (Hay Acquisition I Inc. 2000) on the impact of accurate Self-Awareness on Self-Management skills they found that...
- People *with* accurate Self-Awareness had...
  - a 49% likelihood of having good Self-Management.
  - a 51% likelihood of *not* having good Self-Management.
- People *without* accurate Self-Awareness had...
  - a 4% likelihood of having good Self-Management.
  - a 96% likelihood of *not* having good Self-Management.

A person with low Emotional Self-Awareness has almost no chance (4%) of having good Emotional Self-Management skills. It is necessary to be aware of our emotions in order to manage them.

Further, research on the impact of accurate Self-Awareness on Social-Awareness (Empathy and Nurturing Relationships) showed similar results. They found that...
- People *with* accurate Self-Awareness had...
  - a 38% likelihood of having good Social-Awareness.
  - a 62% likelihood of *not* having good Social-Awareness.
- People *without* accurate Self-Awareness had...
  - a 17% likelihood of having good Social-Awareness.
  - a 83% likelihood of *not* having good Social-Awareness.

A person with low Emotional Self-Awareness has a high likelihood (83%) of *lacking* Social-Awareness skills. If we don't know what we're feeling, it's hard to recognize emotions in others and accept them.

Emotions Defined
There are several definitions for emotion; for example, "a strong generalized feeling, any specific feeling, any of various complex reactions with both psychical and physical manifestations" (*The American Heritage Dictionary*). The definition that captures simply the essence of emotions is, "emotions are energy in motion." One way to visualize the concept of emotion as energy is shown in Figure 26.

In the Positive, Coherent Area (upper right quadrant), what would be some emotions or mild positive feelings you could write on the low energy positive part of the graph? Some examples might include calm, satisfied, secure. What would be some strong positive feelings or emotions you'd put on the high positive end of the graph (to the right)? Some examples might include cheerful, passionate, and enthusiastic. The rounded peaks are intended to suggest the smooth coherence of positive emotions.

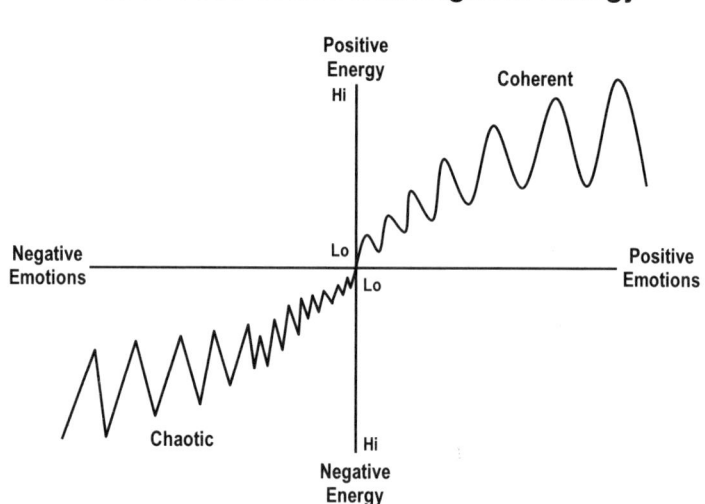

**Figure 26.
Emotions as Positive and Negative Energy**

In the Negative, Chaotic Area (lower left quadrant), what would be some emotions or mild negative feelings you'd associate with low negative energy? How about high negative energy? The spiked peaks are intended to suggest the chaos of negative emotions. Positive emotions boost our energy, while negative emotions drain our energy.

Identifying Emotions and Feelings

The dictionary lists literally hundreds of emotions and feelings. Since it would be difficult and nonproductive to memorize that number of emotions and feelings, we have developed a handy Emotional Self-Awareness Pocket Card (see Figure 27). Part of the card is shown on the following page.

On the pocket card, we've categorized emotions into six simple clusters: Happy, Excited, Angry, Scared, Tender, and Sad. Go to our website (http://www.ByronStock.com/resources.html) to read the instructions on how to download the file and print a card for your own use. Do that now.

Developing Your Emotional Vocabulary

An important part of developing emotional self-awareness is to enhance and expand our own vocabulary of emotions and feelings. Being able to name what we're feeling provides us with information we can use to make decisions about what we should or should not do or say in particular situations. Under each category on the Pocket Card are listed 15-20 emotions or feelings.

CHAPTER 3 — TECHNIQUES   67

Figure 27.
Emotional Self-Awareness Pocket Card

Happy		Excited		Angry	
Amused	Joyful	Amazed	Fearless	Agitated	
Cheerful	Optimistic	Aware	Free	Aggressive	
Certain	Open	Bold	Involved	Annoyed	
Comfortable	Passionate	Brave	Intrigued	Bitter	
Committed	Pleased	Challenged	Invincible	Critical	
Confident	Playful	Courageous	Moved	Disgusted	
Competent	Positive	Curious	Powerful	Enraged	
Delighted	Productive	Determined	Strong	Exasperated	
Encouraged	Proud	Eager	Thrilled	Furious	
Effective	Useful	Energetic		Frustrated	
Flexible		Exhilarated		Hurt	
Free				Impatient	

Using this Pocket Card (or your own memory) for each of the six categories, list on the space provided below two more emotions you personally associate with each of the six categories.

Happy   *Glad* _____   **Excited**   *Thrilled* _____

　　　　　Joyful _____　　　　　　　*Ecstatic* _____

Angry   *Mad* _____   **Scared**   *Terrified* _____

　　　　　Hostile _____　　　　　　 *Worried* _____

Tender *Patient* _____ **Sad**   *Gloomy* _____

　　　　　Loving _____　　　　　　　*Slighted* _____

The ability to identify emotions is crucial. The better we are at naming and discriminating between our different emotions, the better information we give ourselves for decision-making. Our quality of life depends on our ability to discern our emotions, the emotions of others, and then to change our emotions if we want to.

When to Pay Attention to Your Emotions

If emotions are that important, when should you pay attention to your emotions? In what kinds of situations may it be particularly important or helpful to pay attention to what you're feeling? Most people answer, "All the time." Following are some opportunities to practice identifying what you might be feeling. Write your answers to the questions below.

What situations might come up tonight when it would be helpful to pay attention to your emotions? _____

_____

What situations might come up tomorrow? _____

_____

In what past situations might it have been helpful to have paid closer attention to your emotions? _____

_____

The more often we pay attention to our emotions the sooner we'll have information to guide us in our decisions about what to say or do, or *not* say or do.

Emotional Self-Awareness Technique

One simple way to develop your emotional self-awareness skill, and your emotional vocabulary, is to ask yourself:

"What Am I Feeling Right Now?" (WAIFRN)

Notice it doesn't say, "*How* am I feeling right now?" The key is the word "*what*." Practice this technique now. You can use the Emotional Self-Awareness Pocket Card to help you.

What are you feeling right this minute?_____

_____

For example, you might be feeling curious or engaged or challenged. Or, you might be feeling uncertain of what emotions you are feeling right now. You might notice you are feeling two or three emotions at the same time. The Pocket Card can help you identify your emotions.

What were you feeling during your last discussion at work?_____

_____

What are you typically feeling on Monday mornings before going to work?

_____

What are you typically feeling Sunday evenings?_____
_____

Developing the emotional self-awareness skill to anticipate future situations that may cause negative emotions allows you to identify your personal "triggers" and to prepare for them.

Skill Practice Assignment

To improve your skill in this technique, practice asking yourself the question, "What Am I Feeling Right Now?" at least five times each day. This only takes a few seconds. Ask the question both at work and outside of work. Ask it before and after meetings, phone calls, reading emails, listening to voicemails, etc. Don't ask it just when things aren't going well — ask it when things are going well, too. Carry the Pocket Card and refer to it. This will help you expand your emotional vocabulary and enhance your ability to discriminate between various emotions.

The important point is to practice it and get better at it. Remember, the more skilled you are in emotional self-awareness, the easier it will be for you to develop your emotional self-regulation and social-awareness (empathy) skills.

Triggers of Negative Emotions

As you practice the technique, you'll likely begin to notice there are people, events, or situations that frequently "trigger" your emotions, either positive or negative. By recognizing these "triggers," especially those that generate negative emotions, you will know when it might be helpful for you to change or regulate your emotions (the second Emotional Intelligence competency).

Practice Recognizing Emotions and Triggers

For each of the four statements below, identify the emotion and the "trigger" that caused, or led to, the emotion. Circle the emotion and put a box around the trigger.

1. *I feel annoyed when I walk into the family room and see a trail of cookie crumbs from the kitchen to the couch.*

   The emotion is "annoyed," and the situation that triggers this emotion is "seeing a trail of cookie crumbs."

2. *When my daughter rolls her eyes at me, I feel hurt and insulted.*

   Feeling "hurt and insulted" are the emotions. The trigger is not my daughter, but when my daughter rolls her eyes at me. Here is a specific behavior that triggers negative emotions.

3. *I'm getting really angry about all the trivial things the boss has me do.*

   The emotion is "anger." The trigger for the anger is not that the boss has me do things, but rather, *my perception* there are "a lot of trivial things" the boss has me do.

4. *I get muscle tension in my neck on Sunday night just thinking about Monday.*

   An emotion is not stated. Rather, a physical sensation is stated. In this case, "muscle tension in my neck" is the indicator there has been an accumulation of negative emotions (stress) affecting the person's body. It's important to note here, too, that the trigger is simply the act of "thinking," or perhaps more accurately, worrying, about Monday morning.

Our perceptions and our subsequent thoughts can trigger negative emotions in us. By becoming aware of our emotions and their triggers, we can examine our perceptions to determine if they are helpful or harmful.

Identify Your Own Triggers

Turn back to your Personal Goal and Situation Note Sheets (Chapter 2). Review the situations you wrote down, and draw a box around your "triggers." If the trigger is not written, figure out what you think it is, write it down, and box it. These "trigger points" are ideal times to ask yourself the question, "What Am I Feeling Right Now?" In fact, you should ask that question before the trigger occurs, during its occurrence, or after it occurs. The situations you identified in your Personal Goal and Situation Note Sheets are important to you. Becoming more aware of what you're feeling when they occur is the fundamental step in gaining control over your emotions. The point is, by recognizing your triggers and your emotions, you'll have "advance notice" about what's happening to you or what's likely to happen.

What's Important in Your Life?

Now it's time to identify some of the things in your life that trigger positive feelings. In the space below, list those things that are important to your life.

What really matters the most to you? Following each, list two or three positive emotions you feel when you think about these important things. Use your Emotional Self-Awareness Pocket Card to help identify your emotions. For example, one of the things important to many people is family. What would be some of the positive emotions you might feel when you recall your family?

What's Important?   **Positive Emotions and Feelings**

Family   *happy, proud, thankful*

_____   _____

_____   _____

_____   _____

What did you notice about your energy as you listed these important things and the positive emotions they evoke? Do you feel more energized, more positive?

The emotions you listed are what we all want to experience more frequently. They are important to you, your boss, your colleagues, your customers, and your family. The more frequently you think of these things and recall and experience these positive emotions, the more positive your energy will be. When your emotions are positive, thinking is clearer, decisions are better, and your health improves.

Use the WAIFRN Technique
Practice the WAIFRN technique at least five times each day. Carry the Pocket Card with you to refer to so you can expand and more accurately identify exactly what you are feeling. Use this technique at least a week before you move to the next technique — Freeze-Frame.

Coaching/Troubleshooting Notes
Even though you're motivated to use a technique, you may find there are work and life obstacles that seem to get in the way. For each of the techniques taught in this book, there is a list of difficulties people sometimes encounter, with suggested actions you can take to eliminate or minimize them. If you find that you are having difficulty using the WAIFRN technique, find your difficulty on the table below, read the suggestion, and try it out. Give it enough time to have an effect (usually a few days to a

week). If you don't find your specific difficulty listed here, you can email our office to get advice from one of our associates.

Difficulty	Suggestion
• I'm not sure what I'm feeling.	• Use the Emotional Self-Awareness Pocket Card to help you put a name to the emotions you're feeling.
• I seem to feel the same emotions a lot of the time.	• You may, but you also may just need to expand your emotional vocabulary. Use the Emotional Self-Awareness Pocket Card to help you decide if you're really experiencing different feelings. • Pull out your family photo albums. As you look at the pictures, recall and re-experience the positive emotions you had. Use the Emotional Self-Awareness Pocket Card to help you be specific in naming your emotions.
• I forget.	• Write it on your calendar or day planner each day for 2 weeks. When you see WAIFRN, ask the question of yourself and notice your emotions. • Put the stickers (see Free Resources in Quick Information) in several places to remind you.

Key Points
- Emotion is energy in motion.
- By choosing our emotions, we choose whether our energy is negative and chaotic, or positive and coherent.
- When we're managing our emotions we're managing our energy.
- Our quality of life and emotional survival depends on discerning our emotions.
- The technique for building our emotional self-awareness is to ask ourselves, "What Am I Feeling Right Now?"
- When we're in touch with what's important in our life, it boosts our energy.

Summary and Reflection
What would you say if someone were to ask you, "Why is it important for you to be able to recognize stressful events and feelings?"

_____

_____

What are your thoughts and emotions about this section of the book? What did you experience?

_____

_____

What did you learn?

_____

_____

What are you committed to do as a result of what you learned?

_____

_____

TECHNIQUE #2 – **FREEZE-FRAME**®

In This Section You'll Learn:
- How to use the Freeze-Frame technique to eliminate stress and enable you to work more efficiently and effectively
- When to use the Freeze-Frame technique
- When you might find it helpful to "get to Neutral"

Overview
This section will help you learn to use the Freeze-Frame technique to transform stressful feelings and events into positive, productive feelings and actions. In other words, it will help you feel better and do better. This technique develops skill in the first three Emotional Intelligence competencies: emotional self-awareness, emotional self-regulation, and emotional self-motivation. Freeze-Frame is a core technique used to achieve many of the outcomes in the narrative stories, client comments, and quantitative results described in Chapter 4.

When to Use the Freeze-Frame Technique
The four categories below list some situations in which the Freeze-Frame technique can be used. Read over each of the four categories. You might find it eye-opening to put a checkmark in front of those you experience.

Boss / Peers
- "I'm right, you're wrong"
- Boss jumps down my throat
- Last minute requests occur
- Being "dismissed" by boss
- Anxious around executives
- "Because I said so!"
- Bosses don't walk-the-talk
- My requests are turned down
- Inequitable responsibilities and recognition exist
- Executives make snap decisions without discussing them
- I feel micromanaged, frustrated
- Impromptu discussions with executives

Personal
- My "hot button" is pushed
- I doubt my abilities
- I can't concentrate on tasks
- Multitasking
- Public speaking
- To prioritize work
- Needing things to be perfect
- Restructuring is announced
- Before/during a presentation
- Events are out of my control
- Working with people from HQ
- Before/during/after panic attack
- Others perceive me negatively
- Airplane is delayed

Freeze-Frame is a registered trademark of the Institute of HeartMath.

- I feel tense in my neck/shoulders
- I'm afraid to speak up
- I lose focus

- Before/during/after traffic
- I replay events in my head
- During negative self-talk

Direct Reports
- Small events trigger a reaction
- Difficult meetings happen
- I notice I'm talking louder
- People don't seem to care
- During interruptions
- People don't follow through
- Subordinate makes a blunder

- I have to discuss performance problems
- My authority is challenged
- I find out my team is late
- Others don't meet expectations
- I'm peppered with questions
- I see "politics"
- Someone shares gossip with me

Family
- Arguments happen at home
- In-law visits
- Parents are ill/failing
- I think about work at home
- Children act up
- Talking about spouse's job
- Shopping with my spouse

- Teen moves in "slow motion"
- I visit Dad in adult care home
- Family conflict
- Before singing in church
- Teens not doing chores
- Disciplining a child
- Driving with my spouse

You may notice the lists above are similar to or the same as several of the situations for using the "What Am I Feeling Right Now?" technique. As you learn about the Freeze-Frame technique described on the following pages, you'll see why these two techniques go hand-in-hand.

The Freeze-Frame Technique

"The Freeze-Frame technique is a one-minute power tool for transforming stressful or distracting thoughts and emotions into clarity, allowing you to take efficient and effective action. With practice, you will gain more power to come into balance and quickly change a negative, draining response into a proactive, creative one" (Institute of HeartMath pg. 30).

The term "Freeze-Frame" comes from the concept that our life is a movie and we can choose to "freeze the frame" to examine any part of it we like. If you're concerned about it taking one minute, don't be. When you first learn and use the Freeze-Frame technique it will take a minute or so. But as you practice, you'll get faster and faster. After a week or so, you'll be able to do it in just 10–20 seconds, without anyone even knowing it. With continued practice you'll do it even faster.

The Five Steps of the Freeze-Frame Technique
1. Take a "Time-Out"
2. Shift Your Focus to the Area Around Your Heart
3. Activate Positive Feelings
4. Ask Yourself, What Would Be a More Effective Response to this Situation?
5. Listen to Your Heart; Sense any Change in Perception or Feeling

*1. Recognize the stressful feeling. Take a **Time-out** so you can temporarily disengage from your thoughts and emotions — especially stressful ones.*

Sports teams take a time-out. Why? To take a break, to select a better strategy to deal with the current situation, to regain energy, or refocus their attention. In this step, recognize when you're feeling stressed or anxious or angry, and take a time-out. The idea is to stop the action, stop the movie of your life and change/improve what is happening. The shorthand version of this step is "**Time-out.**"

*2. **Shift** your focus to the area around your heart. Feel your breath coming in through your heart and out through your solar plexus. Breathe this way a few times to keep your focus there for ten seconds or more.*

When you're first learning this technique, shift your focus to the area around your heart for about ten seconds. Let me show you how easy this is. Read the three statements below and then close your eyes and do each one for about ten seconds.
- Shift your attention, your focus, to your right big toe.
- Now shift your attention to your right elbow.
- Lastly, shift your attention, your focus, to the area around your heart in the center of your chest.

If you're like the vast majority of the clients in our development programs, you can make the shift to the area around your heart quite easily. The shorthand version of this step is "**Shift**."

3. Make a sincere effort to activate positive feelings. (This can be a genuine feeling of appreciation or care for someone, some place or some thing in your life.)

The key is to activate or engage the feeling, the emotions you had during fun times in your life. What are some wonderful times or experiences in your life you'd like to re-experience? Recalling those times, what emotions were you feeling then? You can use your Emotional Self-Awareness Pocket Card to help you identify your emotions.

In the space provided below, list three wonderful experiences you've had. Beside each one, recall and list the positive emotions you felt then. As you do this activity, put yourself back in that situation or place, and really feel the emotions all over again.

Fun Times	**Positive Emotions and Feelings**
Ex: Sunset over the lake	*happy, relaxed, calm, thankful*

The key to this step is the emotions and feelings. Find that wonderful time in your life, put yourself back there, ask yourself, "What Am I Feeling Right Now?" and then, re-experience those feelings. When you're first learning the technique, you should stay in this step for approximately thirty seconds. The shorthand version of this step is "**Activate.**"

4. Now, **ask** yourself, "What would be a more efficient, effective attitude or response to the situation — one that will minimize future stress?"

This is the simplest step. In this step you are tapping into your wisdom and intuition to guide you. The shorthand version of this step is "**Ask.**"

5. Sense any change in perception or feeling and sustain it as long as you can. **Listen** to your heart.

The key here is to listen. Most of us are so busy we think we don't have the time to listen. We think we have to rush an answer. Your ability to get an answer is in direct proportion to your willingness to listen to your own wisdom. Clients tell us the answer is typically not a loud, booming answer, but a quiet confident one. The shorthand version of this step is "**Listen.**"

Freeze-Frame steps reprinted with permission of the Institute of HeartMath.

Example Using the Freeze-Frame Technique

Since you can't "look at" the Freeze-Frame technique or "hold it in your hand to examine it," the next best thing I can do to "show you" is to give you an example of what goes on for me when I use the Freeze-Frame technique.

I'm sitting at my desk in my office. The situation I'm facing is the looming deadline of getting a proposal done by this coming Friday morning. I notice feelings of anxiety and decide to stop what I'm doing and take a time-out to do something about it. This is Step 1: recognizing the stressful feeling and taking a **Time-out**.

I close my eyes to shut out distractions. I shift my focus to the area around my heart. In my mind, I see my eyes looking at the center of my chest. I see a soft white luminous glow in the center of my chest (but that's just me). Next, I make sure I'm breathing in a nice smooth, deep rhythmic pattern. I focus on the area around my heart and do my breathing for about 10 seconds. This is Step 2: **Shift**.

Next, I say to myself, "Recall some positive, fun times you've had in your life, and activate those feelings." Then some situation or person pops into my awareness. For example, I see Ella, my three-year-old granddaughter. Yesterday she and her sister Abby were visiting us and playing in a little inflatable swimming pool. I can see her smile as her big sister splashes the water on her. I ask myself, "What Am I Feeling Right Now?" (I've already put myself back into the situation.) I listen. I hear, "Thankful, happy, blessed." So, I just soak in those wonderful feelings while I "watch" Ella and Abby in the pool. After a little bit, another scene pops into my mind. I'm riding on my motorcycle out among the orchards, vineyards, and cornfields of Southwest Michigan near my home. I feel the wind on my face, the sun on my arms. I ask myself, "What Am I Feeling Right Now?" I hear, "Relaxed, peaceful, happy, energized." Again, I soak in those wonderful feelings as I "watch" the vineyards, orchards, flowers, and horses go by. This is Step 3: **Activate** positive feelings.

Now, I ask myself, "What would be a more efficient, effective attitude or response to the situation, one that will minimize future stress?" This is Step 4: **Ask**.

I wait. Within a few seconds I hear, "You can do this. No need to be anxious. Focus and get it done." The thought comes to me, "Yes, that's right. No need to worry." So I don't. I let go of the anxiety. This is Step 5: **Listen**. Then I get back to work.

Of course, I don't always recall how I feel about Ella or riding my motorcycle when I use the Freeze-Frame technique. Usually something that has occurred in the past few days or weeks pops into my mind. If it doesn't, I make a conscious choice to go back to some wonderful times from my more distant past — last month, last year, several years ago.

Shorthand Version of the Freeze-Frame Steps
1. Time-Out
2. Shift
3. Activate
4. Ask
5. Listen

Memorize the Steps
For you to effectively use the technique, it is necessary to remember the steps and their correct sequence. In the space provided below, write the shorthand version of the steps four times. Practice recalling them in the right order, and then quiz yourself to see if you spot any step out of order. Memorize the steps now. Write the shorthand version of the steps below.

_____ _____ _____ _____

_____ _____ _____ _____

_____ _____ _____ _____

_____ _____ _____ _____

_____ _____ _____ _____

First Practice
Now that you have the shorthand version of the Freeze-Frame technique steps memorized, practice using it with the Freeze-Frame Practice Sheet on the following pages:

First, read the SAMPLE completed Freeze-Frame Practice Sheet. A sample "job stress" is written, along with sample thoughts and emotions. In addition, since this is a sample of a completed Practice Sheet, a sample answer from using the Freeze-Frame technique is shown under "Coherent Perspective."

Now for your own practice, locate a blank Freeze-Frame Practice Sheet following the SAMPLE. Think back to your Personal Goal and Situation Note Sheets (Chapter 2). There likely will be some job stresses described in those situations. Write three or four words about one real job stress you're having under "job stress."

Next, write six to eight words that represent your thoughts and emotions about the situation. What have you been thinking and feeling about this job stress? When you're done, put your pencil down.

Next, refresh your memory on the five shorthand steps for the Freeze-Frame technique (**Time-out, Shift, Activate, Ask, Listen**).

Now, close your eyes, take yourself through the five steps of the Freeze-Frame technique. When you get an answer in Step 5, write it under "Coherent Perspective." DO IT NOW.

SAMPLE   Freeze-Frame Practice Sheet

Briefly describe the problem, stressor, issue, or situation

Volume of work

Write what you are feeling and thinking

Overwhelmedd, scared, worrying, incompetent, can't focus

Is it me? Maybe I should look for another job?

> Stop and apply the Freeze-Frame technique NOW

Coherent Perspective

Pick the most important item and finish; then do the next one

Adapted with the permission of the Institute of HeartMath

Freeze-Frame Practice Sheet

Briefly describe the problem, stressor, issue, or situation

_____

_____

Write what you are feeling and thinking

_____

_____

> Stop and apply the Freeze-Frame technique NOW

Coherent Perspective

_____

_____

Adapted with the permission of the Institute of HeartMath

Freeze-Frame Practice Sheet

Briefly describe the problem, stressor, issue, or situation

_____

_____

Write what you are feeling and thinking

_____

_____

> Stop and apply the Freeze-Frame technique NOW

Coherent Perspective

_____

_____

Adapted with the permission of the Institute of HeartMath

Debrief: First Use of the Freeze-Frame Technique
What are you feeling right now? Write the feeling(s) in the margin below your "Coherent Perspective" on the previous page. Most people feel calmer, more relaxed.

Look at your completed Freeze-Frame Practice Sheet and read what you wrote under "What are you feeling and thinking?" Think of one or two words that describe your feelings and thoughts. Typical words include: frustrated, overwhelmed, negative. Write the word in the margin on the Freeze-Frame Practice Sheet and circle it. Read what you wrote under "Coherent Perspective." Think of a word that describes your answer. Typical words for this include calm, positive, in control. Write the word in the margin on the Freeze-Frame Practice Sheet and circle it.

Typical Answers of Program Participants
When we have participants in our developmental programs practice their first use of the Freeze-Frame technique, we ask them to share their "Feelings and Thoughts" word and their "Coherent Perspective" word. Below is a sample of words participants tell us:

Feelings and Thoughts	Coherent Perspective
Frustration	Calm
Angry	Focused
Overwhelmed	In control
Leave	Resolved
Confused	Clarity
Hostile	Professional
Powerless	Determined
Defeated	Confident

What do you observe or notice about the two lists of words? Most people say they look like opposites — negative for the "Feelings and Thoughts" and neutral or positive for the "Coherent Perspective." What do you observe or notice about your words for "Feelings and Thoughts" and "Coherent Perspective?" Will the positives you wrote under "Coherent Perspective" be a more efficient and effective response to this particular situation? Will it minimize the stress you were experiencing?

What You Accomplished
In a very short period of time — a minute or so — by using the Freeze-Frame technique, you were able to transform a situation that was frustrating, upsetting, depressing, threatening, worrisome, uncertain, uncomfortable, into

a positive, productive emotional state that will lead you to productive action. With practice, you can transform negative, draining emotions into positive, productive ones in a matter of seconds whenever you want. Not only will you feel better, you will have cleared your mind so you can identify alternatives that are best for you. You'll have changed the chaotic rhythm of your heart into coherent signals that bring balance back to your respiratory and hormonal system. You accomplished this in a few seconds simply by choosing to use the Freeze-Frame technique.

I Know What You're Thinking

The most common concern is, "I just can't see myself closing my eyes and taking a minute when I'm talking with someone or in a meeting." Certain times are easier than others for a new user of the Freeze-Frame technique. We'll be pointing these out after the practice pages in the paragraph entitled "When to Use the Freeze-Frame Technique," along with other helpful suggestions as you begin to use the technique in real-time situations.

Choose those easier times when you first begin. After you practice for a while, you'll be able to use the technique with your eyes open while you are in a meeting or talking on the phone. The idea is to practice until you can do it while you're talking with another person.

Second Practice

The Freeze-Frame technique is *the* critical technique necessary to achieve all of your Personal Goals. Therefore, you must practice. Use another blank Freeze-Frame Practice Sheet. Select a different job stress (or personal stress) and complete the Practice Sheet:

> Write three or four words about a real job or personal stress you're having under "Problem, Stressor." Think back to your Personal Goal and Situation Note Sheets. There are likely to be other job or personal stressors described in those situations.

> Next, write six to eight words that represent your "Feelings and Thoughts." In other words, what have you been thinking and feeling about this job stress? When you're done, put your pencil down.

> Now, refresh your memory on the five shorthand steps for the Freeze-Frame technique: Time-Out, Shift, Activate, Ask, Listen.

> Close your eyes and take yourself through the five steps of the Freeze-Frame technique. When you get an answer, write it under "Coherent Perspective." DO IT NOW.

Debrief: Second Use of the Freeze-Frame Technique

Now that you've completed your second practice of the Freeze-Frame technique, what are you feeling right now? Write what you're feeling in the margin below your "Coherent Perspective."

Did you use the same situations and feelings in Step 3 as you used in your first application of the Freeze-Frame technique, or did you have other situations and positive feelings come to you? Was it faster or easier for you to go through the technique this time? Did you notice it was easier to recall the five steps? Was this stress as significant and as strong as the first one?

When applying the Freeze-Frame technique, you may use different experiences and different emotions to come up with the "Coherent Perspectives" that are best for you. Almost every time you use the Freeze-Frame technique, you'll get an answer that will minimize your stress and make you more effective at work and in your relationships.

What If I Don't Get an Answer?

Once in a while an individual may not get an answer the first time they use the Freeze-Frame technique. That doesn't mean they're doing it incorrectly. It simply means they need more practice. One suggestion is to spend more time in Step 3, re-experiencing wonderful times in your life and the positive emotions you were feeling then. The key is feeling the wonderful, positive feelings. Another suggestion is to slow down, relax, and don't "force" an answer. You have all the answers you need inside of you. Stress just restricts your ability to hear the answer that is best for you. Allow the positive emotions to synchronize with your brain waves so you can "hear" the best answer for you.

The Practice Sheet

Some people ask whether they have to use the Freeze-Frame Practice Sheet. The answer is no. We just have you use it in the beginning so you can see (and record) the differences before and after using the technique, when it's not a stressful situation.

Other Ways to Use the Freeze-Frame Technique

As you learned in the Science section recalling and re-experiencing positive emotions (which is what you do in Step 3 of the Freeze-Frame technique) enables you to think clearly and have full access to your intuition, wisdom, and everything you know. And though many people use the Freeze-Frame technique during times of stress or when they are experiencing negative emotions, you can use the technique when you are not stressed to experience increased mental clarity. By simply changing the question you ask yourself during Step 4, you can use the technique to help you in a wider variety of situations.

For example, let's say that you are about to go into a meeting and you don't feel or anticipate feeling any negative emotions. You can use the Freeze-Frame technique and ask any one of the following questions during Step 4 before you enter the meeting:
- "What is the best thing I can do to make this meeting productive?"
- "What is one thing I can do to make this an effective meeting for everyone?"
- "What is the most important thing we need to accomplish during this meeting?"
- "What is the one thing I can say to demonstrate that I appreciate the complexity of the other teams' jobs?"

You can use the Freeze-Frame technique in this manner for a wide variety of situations both work and personal. Following are a few sample situations when you can use the Freeze-Frame technique this way:

Work
- A coaching session
- Advising your boss
- Giving an assignment
- A performance review
- Meeting a new person
- Writing an email
- Discussing a performance problem
- Interviewing a candidate
- Calling a customer
- Attending a training session

Personal
- Discussing report cards
- Planning a vacation
- Discussing chores with kids
- Doing financial planning
- Discussing health problems
- Talking with kid's teachers
- Attending a recital
- Giving advice
- Talking with a builder
- Attending a church meeting

It is important to think of a question that is relevant to the situation and one that is specific. To make it specific, choose adjectives like "one," or "best," or "most." In addition to using the technique in this manner before a meeting, you could also use it during and even after those situations.

When to Use the Freeze-Frame Technique

There are three main times when you can use the Freeze-Frame technique. They are...
- Before a situation/event
- During a situation/event
- After a situation/event

Before As a new user of the Freeze-Frame technique, the best (and easiest) time for you to use it is *before* a situation. By using the Freeze-Frame technique before a situation you think may or may not be difficult, you prepare yourself to think clearly, be calm and fully present. This will help to keep you from getting "emotionally hijacked" during the event and allow you to tap into your intuition for the best way to handle whatever comes up. For example, you can use the Freeze-Frame technique before...
- A meeting
- A phone call with a customer or colleague
- Responding to or even reading an email
- Listening to your voicemail
- Walking in the door at home after work
- Giving or receiving a performance review
- Talking to your child about her/his grades
- Driving in traffic

It's best to use the Freeze-Frame technique before a situation because you can be in control of the environment in which you use it. You can take as much time as you like. You can have your eyes closed if you wish. As you practice, you will find you can get to the positive emotions and to your answer more quickly. I know it's fun to stay in Step 3, feeling positive emotions, but if you experiment a little, you will find it is possible to get an answer in shorter and shorter time.

After The second best time to use the Freeze-Frame technique for people who are just learning is after a situation. You can use the Freeze-Frame technique after the same situations as you're "before" situations. Why would you use the Freeze-Frame technique *after* a situation? Because you may experience negative emotions or feelings even though you didn't expect you'd be having them. You don't want to let any lingering negative emotions affect you, right? So, use the Freeze-Frame technique to transform them into more positive, productive action and behavior. Again, you can be in control of the environment and take as much time as you like after an event.

During After practicing the Freeze-Frame technique before and after situations for about a week, start using it ***during*** situations. For example, use it during a phone call, or a team meeting, or during a conversation. It would be a good idea to start by using the Freeze-Frame technique during a phone conversation because in this situation you have some degree of control over your environment (no interruptions and no one watching you). That way, if you choose to, you can have your eyes closed to shut out visual distractions while you use the technique. Then you can go on to use it with your eyes open, focusing your eyes on a spot on the floor or wall.

In a meeting, focus on a spot on a wall or on the table. Put any worry of "missing something important" out of your mind. By now, the Freeze-Frame technique will only take you a few seconds. Go through the steps with focus and confidence. Once you get your answer, you will be in a much better mental state to contribute to the meeting.

Identify When to Use the Freeze-Frame Technique

Turn to your Personal Goal and Situation Note Sheets (Chapter 2). Review the situations for each of your Personal Goals and identify times when you could use the Freeze-Frame technique "before," "after," and "during" situations to help minimize your stress, improve the clarity of your thinking, and be more productive. List those times under the appropriate header below. Be specific — give the name of the person or name of the meeting, event, or situation.

Before These Situations:

_____ _____ _____
_____ _____ _____
_____ _____ _____

After These Situations:

_____ _____ _____
_____ _____ _____
_____ _____ _____

During These Situations:

_____ _____ _____
_____ _____ _____
_____ _____ _____

Stickers: Reminders to Use the Techniques
Download the electronic file from our website and use it to print on standard 1" x 2" adhesive labels. See Free Resources in Quick Information section (http://www.ByronStock.com/resources.html). Put the Freeze-Frame stickers in your day planner, near the telephone, on your computer, on the refrigerator, or dash of your car.

A Timely Reminder
At the bottom of the sheet of stickers, there are some circles about ¼" in diameter. Cut out one of these small circles. Or, you can simply use a hole-punch to cut out the adhesive circle. Stick the circle on the center of your watch face. If you don't have a watch, put it on your cell phone or pager or the handset of your telephone at work. Whenever you see this sticker, ask yourself this question, "Is now a good time for me to use the Freeze-Frame technique?" Consider putting the remaining circles on your other personal electronic equipment (computer, cell phone) to remind you.

Eyes-Open Freeze-Frame Technique
As you practice using the Freeze-Frame technique before and after various situations, you'll find you can do it more and more quickly. After a week or so of practicing "before" and "after" situations with your eyes closed, start opening your eyes to do them. Focus your eyes on a spot on the wall or a spot on a table. The more you practice, the faster and easier this will become. After a week or two, you can complete the Freeze-Frame technique in fifteen or ten or even five seconds with your eyes open. When you get to this point, no one will even know you're using it. And after using the Freeze-Frame technique regularly for a month or so, you're likely to find you're becoming "unconsciously competent" in using it. That is, you can use the technique without even consciously focusing on the five steps. You'll have developed new neural circuitry in your brain, a new chosen way of responding to situations that, in the past, were stressful or difficult for you.

Use the Freeze-Frame Technique
Use the Freeze-Frame technique daily, at least five times a day, whether you are at work or home. Your list of situations or events for "befores" and "afters" are the best times because these are the situations that are keeping you from achieving your Personal Goals.

Getting to Neutral
When you're new at using the Freeze-Frame technique, you may find occasions in which you want to use the technique during a situation even if you've not practiced it very much. In these situations, you may find you're able to take a Time-Out (Step 1) and *Shift* your focus to the area around your

heart (Step 2). But, try as you might, you might find it difficult to Activate positive feelings (Step 3). If you can only get to Step 2, you have gotten yourself into what we call Neutral. The power of being able to shift into Neutral has significant benefits.

Shifting to Neutral...
- Saves energy
- Keeps degenerative hormones from flowing through your system
- Prevents wear and tear on your nerves
- Decreases aging of your cells
- Lessens the strain on your heart

Getting to Neutral can be used anytime you feel yourself reacting negatively. Getting to Neutral involves two simple steps: Heart Focus and Heart Breathing. As with the Freeze-Frame technique, you focus your attention in the area of the heart. Then you breathe through the heart area in a steady gentle rhythm.

Neutral is not a substitute for the Freeze-Frame technique, but it is an effective approach anyone can use to help get through difficult situations.

Coaching/Troubleshooting Notes
If you notice you're experiencing trouble in using the Freeze-Frame technique, find your difficulty in the table below, read the suggestion, and try it out. Give it enough time to have an effect (usually 2 weeks). If you don't find your specific difficulty listed here, you can email our office to get advice from one of our associates.

Difficulty	**Suggestion**
• I'm only doing one or two a day.	• Use it before every meeting you attend. Even if you are running late, investing 30 seconds to be calm and have improved mental clarity will make you and the next meeting more effective. Stop and do it in the hallway, stairway, empty room, bathroom, etc. • Use it before each phone call you make or email you write — whether you are anxious or not. Notice how this calms you, and enables you to think more clearly and have more effective communications.
• It's hard to do during a discussion.	• This is typical of new learners. Practice using it before and after discussions, meetings,

	phone calls, etc. Then practice doing it with your eyes open. Build up to using it during meetings and one-on-one conversations.
• It's hard to do when I'm put on the spot.	• See above. • Ask for a time-out during the discussion or meeting. • Tell the person you need to take a minute to think about it. • Ask for a break in the discussion. • Reschedule the discussion.
• I don't have enough positive emotions and wonderful times for Step 3.	• Pull out your family photo albums. As you look at the pictures, recall and re-experience the positive emotions you had. • Take family or vacation pictures to work and put them on your desk, wall, or in your day planner, calendar or computer screen saver. • Write down a list of wonderful times in your life. Behind each one, recall, re-experience, and write down the positive emotions you had.
• I keep using the same people and things in Step 3.	• It's OK to use the same things as long as you can identify the emotions they evoke. • Use scenes or situations in nature. Recall the beauty of spring flowers, an orange sunset, or birds singing at sunrise. • Pull out your family photo albums. As you look at the pictures, recall and re-experience the positive emotions you had.
• I'm not taking the time to do them.	• Look at your Personal Goal and Situation Note Sheets and the situations you identified. How would you benefit by using the Freeze-Frame technique? • Review the Client Comments in Chapter 4 about their use of the technique and the benefits they've received from using it.
• I forget.	• Write the words "Freeze-Frame" or "FF" on your calendar or day planner each day for 2 weeks. When you see FF ask the question "Is now a good time to use the Freeze-Frame technique?"

- Put the stickers (see Free Resources in Quick Information) in several places to remind you.

Key Points
- The Freeze-Frame technique can be used to transform stressful feelings into positive, productive emotions and behaviors.
- Start using it before and after situations. Build up to using it during situations.
- Getting to Neutral is a way to save your energy during difficult situations.

Summary and Reflection
What would you say if someone were to ask you, "What does using the Freeze-Frame technique do for you?"

_____

_____

What are your thoughts and emotions about this section of the book? What did you experience?

_____

_____

What did you learn?

_____

_____

What are you committed to do as a result of what you learned?

_____

_____

TECHNIQUE #3 — APPRECIATION

In This Section, You'll Learn:
- The impact of appreciation on typical business situations.
- How to use the Appreciation technique.
- When to show appreciation.

Overview
This section helps you learn to demonstrate appreciation to other people for their consistent or improved performance, or for their unexpected initiative and effort.

Showing our appreciation to others is one of the key techniques we can use to build our empathy skills, the fourth of the five Emotional Intelligence competencies. The Science section (Chapter 1) explains how feeling and expressing appreciation significantly impacts heart rhythms, brain function, mental clarity and health.

When to Express Appreciation
Look over the categories and situations below to identify when you could express Appreciation. Show Appreciation when…

Boss / Peer
- My boss gives me a heads-up
- A colleague helps me
- My boss clears an obstacle
- I get advice on my career
- I see a good role model
- I get helpful feedback
- I get helpful advice from a colleague
- My boss gives me time to make an important decision
- Boss clearly lays out her/his expectations
- Someone gives me input on a presentation
- Someone reassures me my decision was a good one

Direct Reports
- An employee is struggling
- Someone sits in a meeting for me
- My team beats its deadlines
- Someone volunteers
- At beginning or end of my staff meeting
- I get a polite email reply to my requests
- Someone consistently does a task as expected
- A project is under budget
- A poor performer does something well
- Subordinate does a good job with my boss
- Subordinate crafts a well written press release

Personal
- Customer Service actually helps
- A friend listens while I complain
- Someone gives me a gift
- Neighbor helps my parents
- My assistant reminds me of an important date
- The waiter remembers my special request
- Friends help out during illness

Family
- My spouse helps me
- My teen does what I ask
- Spouse runs errands for me
- My son-in-law helps with a project
- My spouse listens to me complain
- My spouse surprises me with a gift
- The nursing staff does something special for my mom/dad

Why Demonstrate Appreciation to Others?

When we examine the definition of the word "appreciate" in the dictionary (*The American Heritage Dictionary*) we find several meanings, including:
- Grasp the nature, worth, quality, or significance of something
- Value or admire highly
- Judge with heightened perception or understanding
- Recognize with gratitude
- Increase the value of something or someone

Timely, consistent appreciation serves as a powerful motivational tool that helps encourage and sustain valued performance in others. People need to know they and their work are appreciated. Demonstrating genuine appreciation goes beyond the impersonal paycheck or benefits package. People will respond positively to appreciation as long as it's honest, sincere, and deserved. When someone told you they appreciated the work you'd done, how did you feel? How were you affected?

> *The following story provides an example of how sincere appreciation and the use of the Intuitive Listening technique can improve relationships — and performance:*

During Mary's Personal Goal-Setting interview, she shared a situation she identified for the goal of *Managing Emotional Reactiveness*. As finance director of a manufacturing plant, Mary was responsible for getting information from Tom at the end of every month. Tom was argumentative and resisted providing the information she needed. The information was also frequently inaccurate. Needless to say, Mary was quite upset with this because it was her responsibility to provide these financial figures to her Vice President.

In her first coaching session she reported: "Tom has really changed." I reminded her Tom had not attended the training program — she had. I asked what she had done differently relative to her interaction with Tom. She said that before meeting with Tom, she thought about and identified what she could sincerely appreciate about him. At the beginning of their conversation, she expressed her sincere appreciation and then used the Intuitive Listening technique to understand why Tom resisted providing the information. I praised her use of the two techniques and reminded her of what a great job she had done.

Mary was now not only getting the numbers she needed before she needed them, she was also working with Tom to show him how to make the numbers accurate. She went on to say their relationship had improved 1,000% since she started using the techniques — and it began improving during their first conversation after she attended the training!

By expressing appreciation, showing empathy, managing her emotions well, and listening effectively, Mary was able to change a five-months' combative, confrontational relationship into a cooperative, professional one in a single conversation. Subsequently, the information she got was accurate and timely and could be used with confidence by senior leaders in their analysis and decision-making.

Specifically telling someone that you sincerely appreciate what he's done not only feels good, it boosts his energy and increases his self-confidence and motivation.

For a manager, this is one of the best, most effective ways to increase the energy of individuals and teams. It serves to set a positive climate where issues and problems can be discussed with candor and openness.

Improved, Consistent, and Exceptional Performance
When we pay attention to people's work — how they do it and what they produce — it's easy to spot improved, consistent, and exceptional performance. Appreciation encourages the person to continue to put effort, energy, and focus into getting even better. It shows people they and their contributions are important even if they are not exceptional.

Most people in organizations don't always do exceptional things, but they do almost always perform consistently. When occasions or situations present themselves and they really step up and take initiative to help out with a problem or to elevate their performance to the next level, it is very important that you notice and acknowledge that effort. Recognizing exceptional performance reinforces the value of going above and beyond the norm.

The Impact of Appreciation
The power of sincere appreciation is significant and noticeable. Think about the impact of sincere appreciation on:
- Relationships
- Retention of good people
- Productivity
- Initiative/effort
- Customer service
- Adaptability to change

How does sincere appreciation impact relationships? It improves them. What's the impact of appreciation on retaining good people? It's likely to ensure they stay. Appreciation boosts a person's energy level. When people are appreciated they feel happier, confident, respected, committed, competent, proud, and effective. Expressing appreciation is a simple and effective way to positively influence the emotions of others. The point is, appreciation is a very powerful tool we can use to benefit others, ourselves, our department and our organization.

To Whom Can We Show Appreciation?
Since we work with the same people on a regular basis (whether face-to-face, by phone or computer) and live with others daily, we have ample opportunities to notice things we appreciate about them. You can also show appreciation to people you meet as you go about your day or as you travel.

Ineffective or Effective Appreciation
Look at the Appreciation Note Sheet below. Across the first line is an example of ineffective appreciation. In preparing to demonstrate appreciation to Jill, I noted what I appreciated about Jill: She is a "hard worker." "Hard worker" is an inadequate description because it doesn't explain specifically what Jill *did* that deserves appreciation. If we told Jill she was a "hard worker," would she know *what to do again* that deserves our appreciation? No.

Appreciation Note Sheet

Name	Specifically What I Appreciate	Why Valued By Me
Jill	Hard worker	Helped me
Sandy	Stayed late yesterday to get the order done.	Saved me time, helped me keep a promise.

I also note I valued her hard work because it "helped me." Here again, "helped me" is an inadequate description because it doesn't explain specifically how Jill's contribution *supports me*, the department, or the organization. If such information is identified specifically, it strengthens the relationship between us and the other person or between the other person and the organization. On the next line, the effective example for Sandy states much more specifically what we appreciate and why it's valued.

What Do You Appreciate About Your Colleagues and Family?

In the first column above, list each of the members of your team or department. In the second column, write down one thing you sincerely appreciate about each person.

Make sure it's specific. Consider their work, attitudes, initiative, personal and professional qualities. Remember, you can appreciate them for consistent performance, improved performance, and outstanding contribution. In the third column write down why you value that specific performance. How did their actions help you specifically? Now do the same for family members and friends.

Steps to Demonstrate Appreciation
Start by using the Freeze-Frame technique.

Yes, I know you may not be stressed before expressing your appreciation. So why should you start with the Freeze Frame technique? Because the Freeze-Frame technique enables us to get our heart and brain working on the same wavelength (literally) so we can access all the ideas and options in our thinking brain. In the Freeze-Frame process we can ask a question that will help us focus specifically on how to most effectively demonstrate appreciation. For example, you might ask yourself in Step 4 of the Freeze-Frame technique, "What's the best thing I can do to be sincere?" Or, "What specific words can I use that will resonate best with this person?" Or, "What's the best thing I can do to keep from rambling?"

1. State specifically what the person did/does that you appreciate.

This provides the person with the knowledge of what you value and what s/he needs to do again. This information is what you wrote in the middle column of the Appreciation Note Sheet.

2. Explain why you value the person's performance (benefits to you, others).

Even though the person knows what she did that deserves recognition, she does not know specifically why you value the performance or behavior. There could be of variety of reasons. Rather than have her assume or guess, state specifically why or how her performance helps you. This enables her to understand you and what's important to *you*. This information is what you wrote in the last column of the Appreciation Note Sheet.

3. Again, express your appreciation.

Lastly, very briefly, thank the person again for his/her performance.

How to Be Specific
Below are listed some examples of how you can be sure you're being specific when you show appreciation. After looking these over, go back to your list from above and make them even more specific.

Behavior/Performance	More Specific
Completed the report	*Completed the xyz report Monday*
Consistent performer	*Has answered every question I've had about the ABC process*
Always volunteers	*Volunteered in the staff meeting today to get answers from the Marketing department*

Why Valued by Me	More Specific
Helped me	*Saved me 2 hours of work*
Helped the department	*Gave me specific data I could use with my boss to keep from getting our budget cut again*
Helps our customers	*Enabled me to keep a promise I made to Bill at XYZ about a special deliver order*

How Long Does This Take?

Showing your appreciation should not take more than 30 to 60 seconds. If you take longer, there are two likely problems:

- You may be making the person's performance sound more important and valuable than it really is.
- The person may begin to feel you're "blowing smoke," or that you're doing this because you want him or her to do something else.

Either way, that is not the impression you want to leave.

How Would This Person Like to Receive Appreciation?

We've all heard of the Golden Rule, "Do unto others as you would have them do unto you." In terms of appreciation, the Platinum Rule applies: "Do unto others as they would have you do unto them." This means, "How would they prefer to receive your appreciation?" Would she want you to show your appreciation in front of a large crowd or group? Or would that embarrass her? Would he prefer he come to your office, or that you go to his? Or, would she prefer a handwritten note from you, signed and delivered in person?

Shorthand Version of the Appreciation Steps
Use the Freeze-Frame technique
1. Specify the behavior or performance
2. Specify the value to you
3. Express appreciation

Memorize the Steps
In order to be able to use the Appreciation technique whenever you want, you must remember the steps and their sequence. In the space provided below, write the shorthand version of the three steps four times. Practice recalling them in the right order, and then quiz yourself to see if you find any step out of order. Memorize the steps now.
Write the shorthand version of the steps below...

_____   _____

_____   _____

_____   _____

Practice the Appreciation Technique
Now that you have the shorthand version of the Appreciation technique steps memorized, practice using it. Select one of the people from your list and review what it is specifically that deserves appreciation and why that performance is helpful to you. Use the Freeze-Frame process to be calm and to help you think clearly, and then go and show your appreciation. DO IT NOW.

Debrief – First Use of the Appreciation Technique
What emotions are you feeling now? _____

What emotions do you think the person was feeling during and after your expression of appreciation? _____

What did his/her facial expressions and behavior tell you?
_____

Do you think the person is likely to continue doing more of what you appreciated? _____

Were you specific? _____

Did you tell her specifically why it was helpful to you? _____

What's one thing you did really well? _____

What's one thing you would improve? _____

What You Accomplished

In a few seconds, using the Appreciation technique, you were able to show that you pay attention to her and her work and that you value both her work and her as a person. You're also building a stronger relationship with her and relationships are important in getting work done in today's busy environment. With practice, you can do this quickly, showing sincere, honest appreciation whenever appropriate.

Unusual Reactions to Appreciation

Very seldom do clients in our development programs express difficulty in showing their appreciation. Occasionally the feedback we get is that the person who received the appreciation acted like it was no big deal. Some of us are just uncomfortable receiving recognition for our work or for things we have done. Don't let that response deter you from continuing to recognize that person when she or he deserves it. He may outwardly shrug it off, but inside he might be happy as can be.

Another reaction is that a person may act suspicious of your motives for showing the appreciation. This seems to happen more in organizational climates where there is a lot of distrust between people. In that kind of an environment, it may be common practice to "butter someone up" to get him or her to do something. The best advice in this situation is to be very specific and to keep it short and to the point.

Follow the steps and remember to use the Freeze-Frame technique beforehand. This will become one of your trusted techniques, one that not only helps others, but also helps you sincerely feel and show appreciation for those with whom you work and live.

Show Appreciation

You should make a sincere effort to show your appreciation to at least one person a day, whether at work, at home, or in the normal course of your other activities and travels. One of the best things about showing appreciation is that you have to feel it and have it before you can give it away. And in the Science section, you learned the benefits of feeling appreciation on your mental state and on your health.

Reminders to Use
Put the Appreciation stickers you created from the file you downloaded from our website (http://www.ByronStock.com/resources.html) in your day planner, near your telephone, or on your computer. Every time you see the sticker, ask yourself, "To whom can I honestly and sincerely show appreciation today?"

Coaching/Troubleshooting Notes
In the area below, find any difficulty you may be having with this technique, read the suggestion, and try it out. Give it enough time to have an effect (usually about a week).

Difficulty	Suggestion
• It feels unnatural to do it once a day.	• Don't do it when it's not deserved; but also, don't overlook showing appreciation for improved or consistent performance.
• The person seemed ungrateful when I did it.	• Some people believe that is the way to act. They may be suspicious of your appreciation, especially if they hear it only infrequently. Be sincere and show appreciation as they deserve it.
• I forget.	• Write "Appreciation" or "APPR" on your calendar or day planner each day for two weeks. When you see APPR, ask the question, "Whose improved, consistent, or outstanding performance deserves appreciation?" • Put the stickers (see Free Resources in Quick Information) in several places to remind you.

Key Points
- Sincere appreciation has a positive impact on attitudes, morale, effort, loyalty, teamwork, retention and customer service.
- There are many things to appreciate about each member of our team and family.
- Showing appreciation boosts the energy of people.
- Showing appreciation sets a positive tone of cooperation and respect.
- Expressing our appreciation to someone has more impact if we follow a simple three-step process.

Summary and Reflection

What would you say if someone were to ask you, "What does demonstrating appreciation do for you and others?"

_____

_____

What are your thoughts and emotions about this section of the book? What did you experience?

_____

_____

What did you learn?

_____

_____

What are you committed to do as a result of what you learned?

_____

_____

TECHNIQUE #4 — **HEART LOCK-IN**®

Overview
In this section you'll learn to use the power of appreciation to create coherence in your body's biological systems so they operate at peak performance. The Heart Lock-In technique was created by the Institute of HeartMath to help you positively adjust your attitude and restore your energy. The Heart Lock-In technique is key to helping you enhance the fourth Emotional Intelligence competency, Empathy.

Heart Lock-In Technique Helps Your Health
As discussed in the Science portion of this book (Chapter 1), there are documented significant health benefits of sincerely feeling appreciation. At times, participants in our workshops have reported improvements in health-related conditions as a result of regular use of the Heart Lock-In technique. These improvements are anecdotal; not everyone experiences improvements. Most frequently participants report a reduction in sleeplessness. Listed below are some of the difficulties in which participants note improvements. Remember to always follow your physician's advice.

- Sleeplessness
- Anxiety
- Panic attacks
- Muscle tension
- Depression
- Headaches
- Fatigue
- Reduced stress
- Migraine headaches
- Back/muscle tightness

The Heart Lock-In Technique Can Also Be Especially Helpful:
- Before or after sports
- When preparing for a meeting
- When you travel
- When you feel persistent pain
- When preparing for a presentation
- When you feel out of energy

Benefits of Feeling Appreciation
When we feel/experience appreciation (see Science section in Chapter 1):
- Our heartbeats become smooth, rhythmic, coherent, and energy efficient.
- Our hearts and brains become synchronized on the same frequency at about 0.1 hertz, enabling us to think clearly and quickly.
- Our various biological systems synchronize to our heart rhythms and work efficiently.
- Our immune system function, as measured by salivary Immunoglobulin A (IgA), is boosted to protect us more effectively from diseases.

Heart Lock-In is a registered trademark of the Institute of HeartMath.

What Do You Appreciate?

In the space provided, list as many people, situations, events, or good things in your life as you can. Then indicate why you appreciate each one. A few examples are listed.

Who / What?	Why?
Nancy	Wonderful wife, great mother, patient
My motorcycle	The freedom it gives me
Flowers	I feel happy and thankful
Tabor Hill Winery	Peaceful, relaxing setting, good wine

The Heart Lock-In Steps

1. *Focus your attention to the area around your heart.* **Shift** *your focus here.*

   Shifting our focus to the area around our heart enables us to concentrate our conscious attention on the most powerful organ in our body (see Science section, Chapter 1). The heart has the power, when we feel positive emotions, to synchronize with the brain so our heart and brain work together on the same frequency. To help you keep your focus in this area, imagine you're breathing in and out of your heart, taking nice slow breaths in to a count of five; and out to a count of five. You can also put your hand over your heart to keep your attention there. Do this for about 30 seconds. To shut out any distractions in the environment, practice the Heart Lock-In technique with your eyes closed.

2. *Practice sincerely **feeling appreciation** for someone or something in your life as you gently hold your focus in the area around your heart.*

   Feeling sincere **appreciation**, not just thinking about appreciation, creates a dramatic, instantaneous beneficial change in heart rhythm. Recall those people, places, and times in your life that make you feel thankful and grateful. Put yourself back in those situations with those people and feel appreciation for them.

3. ***Send** sincere feelings of **appreciation** to yourself and other people, places, and things.*

   The electromagnetic energy that emanates from the heart each time it beats can be measured eight feet away from our body (Science section, Chapter 1). Couple that with the fact that positive emotions create smooth sine-wave-like heart rhythms, and we can almost see the energy going from our heart to those people, places and things we appreciate. There is also a sense of taking action by "**sending**" our energy of **appreciation**. Do steps 2 and 3 for 10 – 15 minutes total.
   Heart Lock-In steps reprinted with permission of the Institute of HeartMath.

Shorthand Version of the Steps
   1. Shift
   2. Feel appreciation
   3. Send appreciation

Memorize the Steps
In the space provided below, write the shorthand version of the steps three times. Memorize the steps now.

_____   _____   _____

_____   _____   _____

_____   _____   _____

Music and the Heart Lock-In Technique
We all know music has the power to affect our moods and emotions. A good way to keep track of the amount of time we've been doing the Heart Lock-In technique is to use music to help us. Select some instrumental music or music from nature you like, something that makes you feel peaceful, happy, calm, or excited. Determine from the label how much time each song lasts. Play the music in the background as you practice the Heart Lock-In technique. Focus on the Heart Lock-In steps, not the music. You can tell how long you've been doing it by the song being played. I suggest using

HeartMath's CD *Quiet Joy* which includes songs specifically designed to have a regenerative effect on our bodies, mind, and emotions.

It's also a good idea to get a pair of headphones for listening to the music. This helps shut out noise that may distract you from focusing on the steps of the Heart Lock-In technique.

When and Where to Use the Heart Lock-In Technique

The Heart Lock-In technique is used for taking care of yourself emotionally and physiologically. It's not intended to be used in response to stress. Because of this and the fact that I suggest you do it for a longer period of time, it's best to do it outside of work. Listed below are some times of the day and places to use the Heart Lock-In technique. Add times and locations you think will work best for you. Circle the two best times for you and write down where you'll do them.

Morning	**Where**
When I wake up	*Den*
Before leaving for work	*Family room or bed room*
After kids leave	*Rec. room*
Before going into work	*In the car in the parking lot*

Noon	**Where**
Lunch	*My office — door closed*
Lunch	*Conference room*

Evening	**Where**
Before leaving work	*My office — door closed*
Before drive home	*In car in the parking lot*

On the ride home	*Subway car*
Before entering home	*My car in drive way*
After dinner	*On the deck*
After kids go to bed	*Den*
Right before bed	*Family room*

The Long and Short of the Heart Lock-In Technique

In Step 1 of the Heart Lock-In technique, we focus our attention in the area around our heart and imagine we're breathing in and out of our heart. This engages the ANS or "short-term" (vertical) axis.

Figure 28.
Two Physiological Axes of the Heart Lock-In Technique

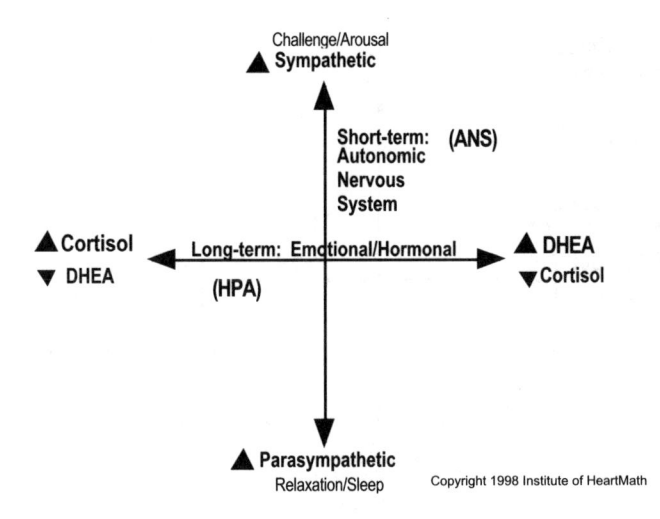

```
                     Challenge/Arousal
                   ▲ Sympathetic
                          ↑
                   Short-term:  (ANS)
                   Autonomic
                   Nervous
                   System
  ▲ Cortisol                              ▲ DHEA
  ▼ DHEA   ←── Long-term: Emotional/Hormonal ──→  ▼ Cortisol
              (HPA)
                          ↓
                   ▲ Parasympathetic
                     Relaxation/Sleep     Copyright 1998 Institute of HeartMath
```

Conscious breathing is a major focus of many meditative practices. Consciously focusing to control our breathing works well, as long as we focus on doing it.

The vertical axis represents the Autonomic Nervous System (ANS). This is the "short-term" access or the "fight or flight/relaxation" axis.

The horizontal or "long-term" axis causes a more lasting effect on our physiology. Two important hormones created in our body are influenced by the emotions we feel. These hormones are Cortisol (known as the stress hormone) and DHEA (known as the anti-aging hormone). DHEA and cortisol are made from the same precursor hormone, pregnenolone. So when DHEA is high, cortisol is low; at these times, you feel younger, more energetic and vital. When cortisol is high, DHEA is low; at these times your energy is low and you may feel older than your years.

The horizontal axis is the HPA or Hypothalamus/Pituitary/Adrenal axis. This is the "long term" axis or the "emotional/hormonal" axis.

How the Heart Lock-In Technique Differs From Meditation

Research has shown the impact of negative and positive emotions on our physiology and bodily functions. Positive emotions lead to higher performance in general. This is a major difference between the Heart Lock-In technique and many meditative practices.

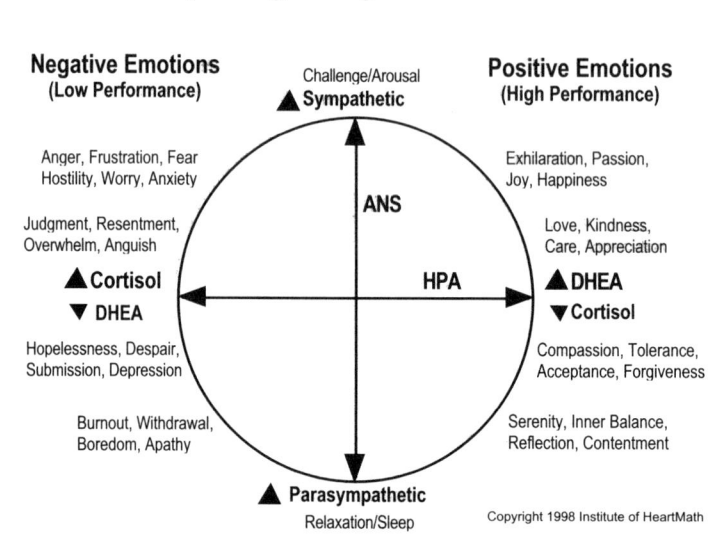

Figure 29.
Two Physiological Systems and Emotions

Negative Emotions (Low Performance)	Positive Emotions (High Performance)
Anger, Frustration, Fear, Hostility, Worry, Anxiety	Exhilaration, Passion, Joy, Happiness
Judgment, Resentment, Overwhelm, Anguish	Love, Kindness, Care, Appreciation
▲ Cortisol ▼ DHEA	▲ DHEA ▼ Cortisol
Hopelessness, Despair, Submission, Depression	Compassion, Tolerance, Acceptance, Forgiveness
Burnout, Withdrawal, Boredom, Apathy	Serenity, Inner Balance, Reflection, Contentment

Vertical axis (ANS): ▲ Sympathetic (Challenge/Arousal) — ▼ Parasympathetic (Relaxation/Sleep)
Horizontal axis: HPA

Copyright 1998 Institute of HeartMath

The Heart Lock-In technique produces both "short term" and "long-term" benefits in our body and in our performance. Meditation practices which do not engage positive emotions, do not typically generate the long-term hormonal benefits. The more negative emotions we feel, the more Cortisol is produced and released into our system and the less DHEA is produced.

These hormones stay in our system for a number of hours, hence, the "long-term" label. These negative emotions lead to lower, poorer overall health and performance.

Physiological Impact of *Negative* Emotions Increased Cortisol and decreased DHEA
- Decreased immune function
- Decreased bone density
- Decreased hepatic function — increased cholesterol
- Abnormal memory and learning capacity
- Increased glucose production

Physiological Impact of *Positive* Emotions Decreased Cortisol and Catecholamine levels; increased DHEA
- Lower heart rate
- Improved heart rate variability (HRV)
- Improved immune function
- Decreased platelet aggregation
- Increased threshold for ventricular fibrillation

Source: The Institute of HeartMath

Practice the Heart Lock-In Technique

Now it's time to practice. Find a quiet place to sit, a place where you won't be disturbed. If you want to use some music to help you know how long you've been doing the technique, get it set up. Get in a comfortable position. Place both feet on the floor, sitting up with your hands resting comfortably in your lap. Review the three steps of the Heart Lock-In technique. Close your eyes and do your first Heart Lock-In technique. Do it for 10-15 minutes. As soon as you're done, complete the debrief questions that follow. DO IT NOW.

Debrief: First Use

Take a few minutes to write your answers to the questions below.

What emotions are you feeling right now? (Use your Emotional Self-Awareness Pocket Card if it will help you.)

_____

_____

What people, places, things, and events did you find to appreciate?

_____

_____

If work or other thoughts intruded on your appreciation, how easy or difficult was it to return to feeling sincere appreciation?

___

___

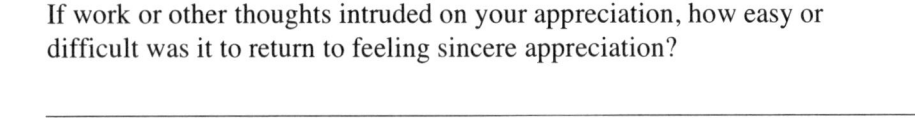

What physical sensations or changes (if any) did you notice while using the Heart Lock-In technique?

___

___

Emotions The most common answers to the first question are "calm, relaxed, peaceful, and energized" or some similar combination. The Heart Lock-In technique seems to have the power to relax and calm us while at the same time energizing us.

People, Places, Things Of course there is a wide variety of people, places, and things we appreciate, some current and some in the distant past. Some of the most powerful emotions come from thinking about our children when they were in grade school or high school.

Work Thoughts Intruding work thoughts seem to occur most frequently when we are trying to use the Heart Lock-In technique at work or early on, when first learning to use it. When you notice you are thinking about work, just gently bring yourself back into feelings of appreciation. What you're trying to do is increase the percentage of time you're in appreciation and reduce the time you're thinking of other things.

Physical Changes Using the Heart Lock-In technique consistently gives us a refreshing break and helps to create higher coherence in our biological systems. That is why you may notice some physical changes while you use the Heart Lock-In technique. People sometimes notice their hands or fingers getting warmer (as circulation flows more freely) or their heart slowing down and becoming more rhythmic.

Difficulties
Typical difficulties clients in our development programs identify with the Heart Lock-In technique include surrounding noises. Surrounding noises disturb concentration. Finding a quiet place and using earphones with music are the obvious solutions for the noise issue.

Once in a while, a participant will find that he focuses on appreciating someone for some specific reason. And then other thoughts creep into his mind that are not pleasant or are disturbing about the person. For example, one client shared with me he thought about his teenage son and how much he appreciated his son. However, other thoughts then came in about having to ground him for something! First, don't focus initially on a person for whom you have highly mixed emotions; focus on other people for whom you generally have positive feelings. Secondly, focus on places you've been, preferably places in nature you appreciate. Places in nature rarely seem to disappoint or cause distraction.

Reminders to Use
Download the file (http://www.ByronStock.com/resources.html) to create stickers and select the "Heart Lock-In" stickers. Put the stickers in places around your home to remind you to use the technique.

Use the Heart Lock-In Technique
In the first hour of sleep, our system is designed for our heart to naturally go into a smooth rhythmic pattern for about a minute or two. This is the same rhythmic pattern the Heart Lock-In technique produces. Practice the Heart Lock-In technique for 15 minutes once a day, five days a week. The 15 minutes can be all at one time or can be two or three shorter segments. By applying the Heart Lock-In technique for 15 minutes, we can significantly increase the amount of time our biological systems are working smoothly and efficiently together. People who regularly use the Heart Lock-In technique frequently report significant reductions in sleeplessness, headaches, and other physical problems.

Coaching/Troubleshooting Notes
In the area below, find any difficulty you may have, read the suggestion, and try it out. Give it enough time to have an effect (usually about two weeks).

Difficulty	Suggestion
• Not making the time to do them.	• On a piece of paper, list the things you do (take a shower, eat breakfast, etc.) and amount of time taken for your morning routine before work and your evening routine. Determine where you can take five, ten, or 15 minutes away from some non-value-added activities. Practice the Heart Lock-In technique at this time. • Combine it with something else you do. For example, when taking a bath soak for ten more

	minutes to do the Heart Lock-In technique.
• I have trouble sleeping or getting to sleep.	• Definitely use the Heart Lock-In technique before you get in bed. Find a comfortable chair, listen to some instrumental music, and use the Heart Lock-In technique. Do this five days a week for two weeks and then notice if you experience an improvement.
• I tried it at work and it was hard.	• Yes, it sometimes is. Do it outside of work. • Find a quiet place where you won't be interrupted. Begin by appreciating yourself and all of the contributions you've made today. Then move into appreciation of other people and things.
• I tried it while out for a walk and it didn't work.	• It's easiest to do the Heart Lock-In technique when you're in a quiet place with your eyes closed. It can be done while you're walking by concentrating on sincere appreciation of what you see in nature. However, this is for the advanced user.
• I'm using the same places and situations and they are losing their emotional impact.	• Pull out your family photo albums. As you look at the pictures, recall and re-experience the appreciation and gratitude you have for those people and places. • Write down a list of wonderful times in your life. Beside each one, recall and re-experience appreciation and gratitude you have for those times and people.
• I forget.	• Write "Heart Lock-In" or "HLI" on your calendar or day planner each day for two weeks. When you see HLI, do a one- or two-minute Heart Lock-In technique right then, and commit yourself to do a longer one when you leave work. • Put the stickers in several places to remind you. • Ask your spouse or significant other to remind you and to help create a quiet environment.

Key Points
- The rhythms experienced while feeling appreciation are the same rhythms our heart goes into in the first hour of sleep to facilitate biological coherence.

- Our heart's rhythms affect other biological systems of our body.
- The Heart Lock-In technique is a simple three-step process.
- Using the Heart Lock-In technique boosts our health and brings synergy to our biological systems.
- Plan when and where to use the Heart Lock-In technique.

Summary and Reflection

What would you say if someone were to ask you, "What does feeling sincere appreciation or gratitude do for you?"

_____

_____

What are your thoughts and emotions about this section of the book? What did you experience?

_____

_____

What did you learn?

_____

_____

What are you committed to do as a result of what you learned?

_____

_____

TECHNIQUE #5 — INTUITIVE LISTENING™

In This Section, You'll Learn:
- How to use the Intuitive Listening technique to make sure the other person feels heard and understood.
- When to use the Intuitive Listening technique.

Objectives
The objectives of this section are to…
- Improve your skill in accurately understanding the meaning another person is conveying to you.
- Make sure the other person feels heard.
- Teach you how to use the Intuitive Listening technique.

Use of the Intuitive Listening technique enhances the fourth Emotional Intelligence skill: empathy. Being able to put yourself in someone else's shoes, to understand not only what they are feeling but also their thoughts and unspoken concerns, is an important aspect of empathy. Demonstrating to people you are talking with that you truly understand them will benefit you and the other person.

When to Use the Intuitive Listening Technique
Samples of situations in which using the Intuitive Listening technique may be helpful are listed below. Put a checkmark in front of situations at work and in your personal life that apply to you.

Boss / Peers
- My boss is upset
- An executive gives me advice
- During a performance review
- In meetings with executives
- When asked to take on a new challenge
- A peer complains about my people
- A colleague and I don't get along
- There are differing opinions (agendas) between people
- My boss gives me a special assignment
- There are conflicts between department heads
- I get feedback on why I didn't get the promotion
- I get criticism instead of helpful feedback

Direct Reports
- People are resisting a change
- Giving a new assignment
- Someone is angry
- Someone second-guesses my
- I want to engage others and get them involved
- A supervisor asks to talk with me
- I want to influence a person or

- decision
- During hiring interviews
- During an exit interview
- Someone objects to my decision
- Planning an agenda with my team
- group
- I'm peppered with questions about a change
- Discussing a political blunder with a subordinate

Personal
- People vent
- During a downsizing meeting
- During Q&A after a presentation
- When mentoring/coaching someone
- People aren't rational
- People interrupt my work
- To keep from interrupting
- A customer complains
- Talking with people from other countries
- Talking with a vendor who lost the contract
- Deepen a relationship with a dealer/customer
- Discussing a proposal with a potential customer

Family
- Arguing at home
- My spouse tells a story
- I treat family as "employees"
- My teen gets in trouble
- My daughter talks about prom
- A friend has a problem
- Discussing financial issues with my spouse
- I'm traveling
- My spouse talks about work problems
- My teen talks about college
- There is an emergency
- Discussing my parents' health problems
- Meeting with an insurance agent
- Talking with a doctor

Demonstrate Your Understanding

Being a good listener is not enough. We must demonstrate to the other person we accurately heard not only what s/he said (the words) and how s/he feels about it (the emotions), but also the meaning underneath his/her words and emotions. Knowing the meaning underneath the words and feelings enables us to really connect. When people are "in sync," each understands the meaning the other person is trying to convey. Our best conversations occur when we sincerely care about the other person. That's what Intuitive Listening enables us to do — engage our whole self in the process of understanding the other person and demonstrate that we do.

Why Intuitive Listening?

There are any number of communication techniques that focus on getting other people to both explain more and feel more comfortable with us as the listener. "Mirroring" (repeating exactly the words the other person said) and

Neuro-Linguistic Programming (matching the exact same body positioning of the speaker) come to mind. They generally focus on something we can do to make the transaction or interaction between us and the other person work to our advantage.

About Intuitive Listening

Intuitive Listening focuses on improving our understanding of the other person by being our authentic self and managing our own emotions during the conversation. The intention in Intuitive Listening is to make sure the other person feels heard and that you, the listener, truly understand the speaker's meaning, not just his words and not just his emotions.

Intuitive Listening starts with your intention to truly try to understand the other person. By setting your intentions and by managing your own emotions during the conversation, you can increase the effectiveness of your listening and show the other person that what he has to say is important. This approach opens the way to transform conversations into strong relationships. Intuitive Listening is the technique you can use to become a transformational leader, transforming all of your conversations into stronger and stronger relationships. Building relationships is not only key to demonstrating empathy (the fourth Emotional Intelligence competency) but also essential to creating trust and loyalty.

Intuitive Listening Motivates Poor Performers

During the initial goal-setting interview and subsequent coaching sessions with Marilyn, I formed the impression she was a firm but fair manager. Marilyn was responsible for about 85 people in a district office of a large government agency. She and her two supervisors where the only ones in the office who were not represented by one of the three unions. Marilyn was new to this particular district office, although she had managed other offices.

Marilyn talked about her "five-percenters." The "five-percenters" are the group of employees in every district office who are poor performers. They typically argue frequently with supervisors and don't want to do very much work. One of Marilyn's Personal Goals was to *Improve her Emotional Reactiveness* in dealing with her "five-percenters."

In her impact interview two months after the training, Marilyn described how she was doing in dealing with her five-percenters. She began by actively initiating conversations with them when they were not in trouble. She used the Intuitive Listening technique to understand them and their situations better, although she seldom agreed with their point-of-view. She started acting more like a coach than an authoritative supervisor. She used the Freeze-Frame technique and Intuitive Listening technique when she met with them to discuss their poor performance. She conducted those conversations with dignity and respect and told me there was no shouting or cussing as in the past.

The atmosphere had changed. (Actually, it was she who had changed the atmosphere.) Marilyn was proud to say she was winning over two of her three five-percenters after only two months. This created a less stressful environment and, because they were actually doing their work instead of complaining about it, they were less of a burden on her "good" employees. She also was proud to point out that, unlike previous managers for that district office, since she came to the office there had been no grievances filed by the five-percenters.

The point of the story is, Marilyn used Intuitive Listening to demonstrate dignity and respect to people who had previously been labeled as "problem employees." The technique boosted her confidence to talk and listen openly and honestly with people about their issues and her own concerns. The bottom line was, Marilyn was getting the five percent increase in manpower she had been missing, and an improvement in the climate and culture that promoted cooperation.

Common Barriers to Effective Communicating

Communication problems account for significant amounts of stress, wasted energy, and resources, both personally and organizationally.

Obstacles to effective communication include...
- Interruptions — the listener interrupts before the speaker has the chance to fully complete his/her communication.
- Distractions — people are unable to effectively listen due to their own distracting thoughts or distractions in the environment.
- No Verification — the listener fails to verify what she thinks she heard — she doesn't ask the speaker to make sure what he really meant.
- Assumptions — the speaker assumes the listener understands jargon or buzz words.
- Emotional Reactions — the listener misinterprets the essence of what the speaker is communicating by reacting to the words at a surface level, rather than the meaning which is being communicated at a deeper/broader level.
- Judgments — the listener forms judgments about the speaker or the content and does not fully listen to what is being said, or he allows his judgmental attitude to bias his listening.

- Fear — the speaker won't say what he wants to say because he is afraid of what might happen to him if he does; or the listener won't ask questions she needs to ask for the same reason.

Is this a representative list of the usual barriers you experience in your workday? What's the impact on you when you don't listen completely and thoroughly to others? Imagine the impact on your relationships and your performance if you could minimize or eliminate just half of these problems during important conversations.

What Makes a Great Conversation?
Try to remember a really great conversation you've had. What were some of the notable qualities or characteristics that made it a great conversation? Common responses to this question include…
- Emotionally, the listeners were neutral to positive
- Each person accurately stated what the other person said and felt
- There were no hidden agendas
- The environment in which conversation was held was quiet
- The listener and speaker felt like they were "in sync"
- The listener and speaker did not feel rushed or hurried

The Chinese Character for "Listen"
The goal of the Intuitive Listening technique is to experience deeper, more effective communication between two or more people. In listening intuitively with the heart, instead of just the head, our goal is to make sure the other person feels heard, allowing for more sincere and effective communication.

Some years ago Bruce Cryer, the CEO of HeartMath, was in Hong Kong teaching the techniques to a group of executives at Cathay Pacific Airways. As he explained the Intuitive Listening technique one of the participants said that it reminded him of the Chinese character for the word *listen*.

**Figure 30.
The Chinese Character for the Word "Listen"**

Labels: Ear, The King, Eyebrow, Eye, One, Heart

After hearing the explanation of the Chinese character Bruce said it should be shown and explained every time the technique is taught. The Chinese character for "listen" summarizes what Intuitive Listening is all about. Intuitive Listening is listening with our ears, our eyes, and our heart, all as one; with the respect we would give a king.

The Intuitive Listening Steps

1. *If you can, before the conversation, use the Freeze-Frame technique, asking the question in Step 4, "What's the best thing I can do to make this an effective discussion?"*

   Using the Freeze-Frame technique beforehand enables us to think more clearly and to calm our emotions before having a conversation. If you don't have time to use the Freeze-Frame technique before your conversation, move on to Step 2.

2. *Actively appreciate the person speaking as you listen for the essence of what he is telling you.*

   In-the-moment, appreciate the speaker. You can appreciate the fact that he is sharing this concern with you. You can appreciate the courage it takes to speak up on this issue. You can appreciate something the person has done in the past or something she has done to help you. Feeling sincere appreciation for the speaker allows you to...
   - Clear your thinking
   - Put yourself in a positive mood
   - Keep your own thoughts from interfering
   - Make you more receptive to hear others

3. *Do not interrupt.*

   If we interrupt the speaker, even if we're trying to help him, it becomes our conversation. We don't get to hear all of the person's story, concerns, or issues. And, unfortunately, it takes the focus off the speaker and puts it on us. We hear and learn more when we don't interrupt, which gives us more insight into the person and the situation.

   And what are you listening for? You're listening for the meaning or essence of the words and feelings, the truth underneath them. One good way to get a grasp on this is to imagine stepping back from the conversation while asking yourself, "What is the real meaning, or truth, or essence underneath these words and emotions?" Pay attention as you listen to determine what that might be.

4. *Verify your understanding by saying something like, "What I heard you say underneath the words and feelings was _____ Is that accurate?"*

When we verify what we thought we understood the speaker to say — the real meaning or truth, or essence — it enables us to be absolutely sure we are accurate. It also shows the speaker we were really listening to her and understanding her. Effective listening, using the Intuitive Listening technique, is a critical foundation skill to experience and demonstrate empathy. Instead of just nodding or saying "I understand what you mean," we actually get confirmation from the speaker that we do, in fact, know what she means.

If you tell the speaker what you understood, and she replies, "Yes, that's what I mean," then allow her to continue to talk. If you're not quite accurate, encourage her to talk some more while you use Steps 2 (appreciation) and 3 (don't interrupt) of the technique. After a minute or two, use Step 4 again to verify what you think she is trying to convey.

When using the Intuitive Listening technique you don't have to worry about being absolutely accurate. Since you're going to verify your understanding, the speaker will help you "home in" on the real meaning. Intuitive Listening steps reprinted with permission of the Institute of HeartMath.

Shorthand Version of the Steps
1. Use the Freeze-Frame Technique
2. Appreciate and listen
3. Don't interrupt
4. Verify

Memorize the Steps
Write the shorthand version of the steps below and memorize the steps now.

_____   _____   _____   _____
_____   _____   _____   _____
_____   _____   _____   _____
_____   _____   _____   _____
_____   _____   _____   _____

When to Use
You can use the Intuitive Listening technique anytime, with the biggest payoff being "high stakes" conversations. Below is a list of some "high

stakes" situations and potential benefits of using the Intuitive Listening technique. Below these samples, list some of your own high stakes opportunities coming up in the next week or two and the potential benefits to you. Go back to the situations you listed under each of your three Personal Goal and Situation Note Sheets (Chapter 2) and use those situations as a place to begin.

High Stakes Situations	**Potential Benefit**
Team disagreement	Demonstrate understanding; show empathy and resolve conflicts
Someone complains	Solve the problem; no more complaints
Advising an executive	Influence decisions; be seen as helpful
Arguments at home	Resolve conflict; relaxing evening
Son's report card	Show your care and support without frustration

Illustration

One of our associates shared a story illustrating the benefits of the Intuitive Listening technique. At the time, Donna was the family's breadwinner. Her husband was completing his degree in chiropractic medicine. One Friday evening after a long week on the road, Donna came home, walked into the kitchen, and Jim, her husband, began to complain, "You're never around! I miss you. I never see you anymore! I have to do everything: take care of Ellie, get her to her school functions, and clean up the dog crap from the carpeting!"

Donna was upset. "I'm the one making the money here! I'm the one putting food on the table!" she thought. She heard a little voice in her head say, "Now would be a good time to use Intuitive Listening." However, another voice said, "I'm the one who's tired here; give me a break!" So, Donna decided to escape from her complaining husband. She left the kitchen and walked upstairs to their bedroom. It didn't work; he followed her.

"Why do you have to travel so much? Ellie's upset and I'm upset with your being gone all the time! I never get to spend time with you. You don't seem to care about all we have to do!" After a minute or two the little voice crept back into Donna's head, "This would be a good time to use the Intuitive Listening technique." This time she did. She shifted into appreciation for Jim, didn't interrupt him, and really tried to understand what was underneath these words and apparent emotions. She thought to herself, "What's he really trying to tell me?"

After a minute or so of really listening to him, she said, "Are you telling me you love me and miss me?" Jim replied, "Yes. And I want you here with us more."

You may be saying to yourself, "I sure wouldn't have gotten that from what he was saying." If you were Donna, and you were appreciating your husband, and you had the intention of truly trying to understand the man you love, I bet you would have. Setting your intention of sincere caring and understanding is a powerful force in helping you cut through words and apparent feelings.

While you're listening, ask yourself, "What's really underneath the words and the feelings being expressed? What's the person really trying to tell me?" Feeling appreciation for the person and not interrupting can enable you to accurately answer these questions.

First Practice
Since Intuitive Listening is about practicing listening, it's a good idea to plan when you're going to use the technique. Select one of your real situations from the list you noted of your High Stakes Situations. Before the meeting or discussion with the person, be sure to use the Freeze-Frame technique. Ask yourself this question (Step 4), "What's the best thing I can do to make this an effective discussion?"

Set your intention to try to truly understand the meaning or truth a person is conveying to you. Allow the person to speak, without interruption, while you sincerely appreciate her. After a couple of minutes, tell her what you think you heard underneath the words and the expressed emotions. Then ask, "Is that accurate?" Depending on her answer, she may clarify what she meant, or she may say, "Yes, that's right," and continue with the conversation.

Continue using the Intuitive Listening technique until the conversation or meeting is over. You'll likely be surprised not only how much additional information you received, but also how much more you understand about her and her situation or issue. As soon after the conversation as you can, complete the debrief activity below.

Debrief Questions: First Use

Do you think the person speaking felt heard? Why? What did she do or say that makes you think so?

_____

_____

Did you find you were able to summarize in a few seconds what it took the speaker two to three minutes to say?

_____

_____

What was the value to you and the speaker of using the Freeze-Frame technique before the conversation?

_____

_____

What benefits did you and the speaker receive by using the Intuitive Listening technique?

_____

_____

What one thing did you do well?

_____

_____

What one thing could you do that would make you even more effective next time?

_____

_____

If you followed the steps in the process, the speaker felt heard. Since you won't seek feedback from the person in this situation, you have to be the judge.

You should have been able to summarize or share the speaker's real meaning in 15–30 seconds, something that took the speaker several minutes to explain. In this process, you're not "parroting" the speaker's words or phrases. You're not trying to tell her the feelings she expressed. Instead, you're trying to get underneath both of those. Not that you won't hear the words and emotions; you will. What you're looking for is deeper than both of those.

It's like sitting back during the discussion and asking yourself, "What do I really think the overall message of this conversation is about?" If you're able to do that, you'll find it takes very little time to verify the meaning or essence with the speaker. One of the advantages of the Intuitive Listening technique is it saves time both in-the-moment and later. Because you really do understand the person and demonstrate your understanding by verifying, she won't feel like she has to explain it to you again later.

Additionally, using the Freeze-Frame technique before listening is likely to relax you, help you focus better, and enable you to feel sincere appreciation and empathy for the speaker.

Common Concerns

Interrupting the Speaker Because we are in such a rush to get all of our work completed and because we have so much work to do, finishing other people's sentences and interrupting them has become the norm. Somehow we have come to believe that by doing this, we can save ourselves and the other person some time. But in these important, high stakes conversations, the best way to save time is not to interrupt; but to hear the person out and show him in fact you do understand him. Interrupting may frustrate the speaker, cause him to lose his train-of-thought, and cause him to feel you are not really interested in listening or helping him.

Difficulty Appreciating Someone with Whom You Have a Conflict For some people, it's difficult to appreciate someone with whom they're currently having a conflict. Try these ideas:
- First, use the Freeze-Frame technique before the conversation and ask yourself, "What are some things I can sincerely appreciate about this person?"

- Second, focus on appreciating that the person has information that may be helpful or valuable to you.
- Third, if it is a difficult situation for the speaker, appreciate the courage it takes for her to bring this issue to your attention.

Talkative People Some of us work with people who can seemingly talk continuously without taking a breath, not providing a convenient stopping point for you to verify what you heard. If you're engaged in a conversation with a person like this, after a few minutes (before you lose your understanding) stop the person and say, "Excuse me for interrupting, but I want to make sure I understand what you're saying. What I'm hearing you say is _____. Is that accurate?" Then, allow the person to continue. After a few more minutes, you may need to stop the person again to express and verify your understanding of the additional information, thoughts, and feelings he expressed to that point.

How Often?
How often should you use the technique? As frequently as you have important conversations at work or at home. If you have a lot of meetings at work you probably could use it several times a day. How about at home? Do you have a spouse or significant other? Do you have children? How often do they need you to really listen and understand them?

Reminders to Use
Don't forget to use the file you downloaded from our website to create the "Intuitive Listening" stickers. Put them in places where you're likely to see them when it will do you (and others) the most good.

Coaching/Troubleshooting Notes
In the area below, find any difficulty you may be experiencing, read the suggestion, and try it out. Give it enough time to have an effect (usually about two weeks).

Difficulty	Suggestion
• I seem to say the same thing the person said to me.	• As you're listening and appreciating the person, imagine in your mind that you step back away from the conversation. Ask yourself, "What's the real message or meaning this person is trying to convey to me? Why is he sharing this with me?" Then, when there is a pause in the conversation, tell the person what you think you're understanding and ask if you're accurate.

• It's hard not to interrupt.	• Yes it is. But it's just a habit. Imagine you have duct tape over your mouth or hold your hand over your mouth. • Focus on appreciating the speaker and what she thinks is important for you to know.
• The person or subject is boring.	• All the more reason to use the technique! You will often gain new information and have a greater appreciation for the person by using the Intuitive Listening technique. • Focus on sincere appreciation of the speaker.
• I forget.	• Write "Intuitive Listening" or "IL" on your day planner each day for two weeks. When you see IL ask the question, "When will I be able to use the Intuitive Listening technique today or tonight?" • Put the stickers (see Free Resources in the Quick Information section) in several places to remind you.

Key Points
- When using the Intuitive Listening technique, we use our ears, our eyes, and our heart all as one and give the person who is speaking the respect we'd give a king.
- The best, most effective conversations occur when people are "in sync." Feeling appreciation is a way for you to get "in sync."
- Thoughts, mismanaged emotions, beliefs, and the setting can get in the way of effective communication.
- Verifying what we thought we heard is the most important part of effective listening.
- Making sure the other person feels heard is critical to effective listening.
- Both the speaker and the listener benefit.

Summary and Reflection
What would you say if someone were to ask you, "Why is the Intuitive Listening technique more effective than other listening techniques?"

_____

_____

What are your thoughts and emotions about this section of the book? What did you experience?

_____

_____

What did you learn?

_____

_____

What are you committed to do as a result of what you learned?

_____

_____

CHAPTER 4

RESULTS

ILLUSTRATIVE STORIES

As promised, the **SMART EMOTIONS** set of techniques presented in Chapter 3 stand on their own merit. In consideration of your valuable time, we offer these true stories simply to add to your enjoyment and motivation as you master the skills. Like the science and research that underlie every technique, you may spend time with them or not as you choose.

During the 12 years I've been teaching the Emotional Intelligence techniques and conducting follow-up coaching, people have shared personal stories illustrating the impact these techniques have had on individuals, teams, and families. The stories shared were not confidential: all of the names have been changed to maintain anonymity.
- Managing Emotions and Getting a Promotion
- News Broadcasts and Impact on Emotions
- Intuitive Listening Eliminates International Resistance
- Using the Freeze-Frame Technique in an Emergency
- Regular Use of Techniques Changes Old Patterns
- What Can Happen When Two Executives Listen to Each Other
- Even the Best-of-the-Best Sales People Can Improve
- Changes in the Boss Impact His Staff

Managing Emotions and Getting a Promotion

For several years I had noticed my friend Jeff seemed to be nervous a great deal of the time in social situations. I thought that was rather unusual, as he worked in sales. Jeff was an account manager for his company's largest customer. As such, his department received a lot of attention from the senior leadership.

I encouraged Jeff to come to an invited development program. Finally, after about four years, he agreed with the whole-hearted support of his wife. When I conducted the one-to-one confidential goal-setting session with Jeff, I learned some things I never would have guessed. Jeff disclosed that he got angry, raised his voice, and even shouted and yelled at customers and people inside his company. This occurred whenever he felt he was under pressure from his customer or was not getting support from internal associates.

Jeff participated in the program actively. The coaching sessions revealed that he was improving in recognizing his emotions and using the Freeze-Frame technique to handle the pressure. He was also doing a good job of remembering to use the Heart Lock-In technique daily. Over the next several months, Jeff seemed calmer. His wife shared with me that she was noticing positive changes in him. Jeff was progressing, so I stopped asking him about his use of the techniques.

> "I never would have gotten this promotion if you had not started me paying attention to my emotions and using the techniques to manage them better. Instead of getting upset, now I'm calm under pressure."

About eight months later, my wife and I were having dinner with Jeff and his wife and other friends. An acquaintance stopped by our table. I introduced him to the people at the table. "Jeff is an account manager for a very large customer of a company here in town," I said. "Actually," Jeff politely corrected me, "I was promoted to Director a couple of months ago."

After my acquaintance left, I apologized to Jeff and told him I was not aware he had been promoted. Jeff stopped, turned, looked me in the eye and said, "I never would have gotten this promotion if you had not started me paying attention to my emotions and using the techniques to manage them better. Instead of getting upset, now I'm calm under pressure. In fact, people remark to me about it all the time. When people around me are falling apart, I calm them down and help them think through the situation." I said, "Jeff, you're the one who used the techniques. *You* earned the promotion." Jeff just smiled.

The point of the story is, Jeff used the techniques to manage his emotional reactiveness to customers' demands and lack of cooperation from internal colleagues to remain calm and to solve problems without blowing up. He went from being the department "hot head" to being "Mr. Calm Under Pressure." Impressed by the significant personal change Jeff had made in handling pressure, the senior management was confident he could professionally lead others and make more important decisions under pressure.

News Broadcasts and the Impact on Emotions

Don is the general manager of a plant for a multi-billion dollar manufacturing company; one of their high-potential leaders. At the end of the Kickoff Session with his group, Don came up to me and said, "I'm real interested in this course. When I attended the Leadership and Change Program at Harvard, we talked a lot about how Emotional Intelligence can impact the culture of an organization and affect the bottom line. But from your description, it sounds like I'm really going to learn some techniques to develop my skills." I told Don he was correct.

During the first day of the program, I taught the group the Heart Lock-In technique and how to use our proprietary software to monitor their progress. Using a fingertip sensor attached to a computer, the software shows real-time heart rate variability data on the screen. The second day, before classes started, Don came walking into the classroom carrying his open computer. He kept saying, "You've got to see this!" to anyone in the room who would listen.

Don explained that, based on our discussion during class, he wanted to see if there was any impact on his emotions as he listened to the news while driving in, as he did every morning.

This morning Don turned his computer on when he got in his car, attached the pulse sensor to his finger, and turned the computer's screen so he could not see his heart rate data. He listened to the news for about 10 minutes as he drove, catching up on the war in Iraq, the new scandals being uncovered with major corporations, etc. Then, out of curiosity, he turned the computer around and looked at the screen. He was horrified. What he saw was a graph of his very chaotic, incoherent heart rhythms. He knew that was not good for his heart, or any other system in his body.

Therefore, he turned off the news and put in a CD of some of his favorite music. Again, he turned the computer around so he could not see the screen and drove the rest of the way to the education center. When he arrived, he stopped the software. What he saw on the screen astounded him: a smoother, more coherent, rhythmic pattern created by the positive emotions he was feeling while listening to the music.

When the session started, Don shared his story with the entire

> **We are often unaware of the real physiological impact of just *hearing* about all the depressing, sad, frightening and irrational events in the world.**

group. After hearing his story, four people remarked they were not going to listen to the news on the way to or from work anymore; they were going to listen to music instead.

The point of the story is, we are often unaware of the real physiological impact of just *hearing* about all the depressing, sad, frightening and irrational events in the world. Proactively choosing to fill our hearts and minds with things that make us happy and light-hearted causes a much greater benefit to our biological systems than we realize.

Intuitive Listening Eliminates International Resistance

Steve is part of an international IT team responsible for convincing franchise owners in Southeast Asia to implement new point-of-sale software for a global company. Although Steve's heritage is Japanese, he grew up and was educated in the U.S. Steve had worked with the Japanese and Chinese for a number of years on other IT projects. He knew that Japanese franchise owners resisted U.S. companies when they came in and proposed changes in local operations. In previous meetings, he noticed a subtle form of resistance that typically caused projects to be delayed by several months. The Japanese franchise owners would say "yes," and politely agree. Then, after Steve flew home, they would not follow through on their commitments and subsequently missed deadlines for implementation.

In Steve's impact interview, he related how he improved the results dramatically. A couple of weeks after taking the course, Steve flew to Japan to meet with the heads of five regions. On the flight over, he used the Freeze-Frame technique to stay calm and focused; he used it to come up with new ideas on how to deal with this subtle form of resistance. He realized the major thing he needed to do was to use the Intuitive Listening technique.

During the meeting, he used the Intuitive Listening technique to hear, demonstrate his understanding and identify the real causes of their resistance. He listened not only to the words and feelings, but also to the silences, the pauses and to his own intuition. He asked questions to help him clarify and see the nuances of their views. Instead of directing and telling them what to do, he surfaced their subtle concerns and honored them as meaningful and valid.

Using the Intuitive Listening and Freeze-Frame techniques, Steve was able to identify and respectfully resolve all of their concerns during one meeting! The outcome was that implementation occurred in a couple of weeks instead of three or four months. Steve was delighted with the outcome and with how well he applied the techniques to help him achieve his desired results.

The point of the story is, when dealing with people and cultures different from ours, listening, rather than telling, is a better way to uncover important subtle issues that are, in fact, make-or-break points. Listening with our whole being and showing respect builds trust, which opens the door to cooperation.

> **When dealing with people and cultures different from ours, listening, rather than telling, is a better way to uncover important subtle issues that are, in fact, make-or-break points.**

Using the Freeze-Frame Technique in an Emergency

I conducted a developmental program on a Wednesday and Thursday and began follow-up coaching sessions by phone the next Wednesday. Participants were managers, supervisors and associates in a government agency. I called Debbie about 2:00 in the afternoon for her coaching session. As I always do, I asked her how she was doing in using the Freeze-Frame technique. She told me she was doing great! I could hear enthusiasm in her voice. I asked her to give me an example of when she had used the technique.

Debbie told me that on Friday evening she was with her husband when he started feeling ill. In fact, he felt so bad they thought he was having a heart attack. She called 911 to get an ambulance. As she cared for her husband and waited for the ambulance, she glanced down at her watch to see what time it was and saw the colored sticker on her watch. It was there to remind her to use the Freeze-Frame technique whenever she felt pressed for time.

She remembered from the class that feeling anxious or worried would keep her from thinking clearly, and she wanted to make sure she was clear and accurate for the paramedics who were on their way. She used the Freeze-Frame technique. In fact, over the course of the rest of the evening and into the late hours of the night, she used the Freeze-Frame technique 15 or 20 times. She said it helped her listen to the doctor and to answer his questions accurately and completely. Then she used the Heart Lock-In technique before going to sleep in the waiting room. She slept well and soundly for about five hours. The next morning, they told her that her husband had not had a heart attack and he was free to go.

The point of the story is, even in an emergency — especially in an emergency — it is important to remain calm, be mentally alert, and retain your ability to communicate information accurately and succinctly. Using the techniques in **SMART EMOTIONS** enables you to do just that.

Regular Use of the Techniques Changes Old Patterns

In September of 1995, I became an independent certified trainer with the Institute of HeartMath. One of the commitments of my contract was to practice the techniques every day, which I did regularly. About six months after being certified, I was

> "I knew the techniques were changing me for the better. My new unconscious response was much better than my old reaction would have been."

flying from Orlando to Newark. Shortly after takeoff, the flight attendant poured my soft drink into a cup and placed it on my tray table. Within a minute, I had spilled the entire cup of soft drink in my lap on my light grey pants. The flight attendant handed me a stack of napkins to soak up the soft drink. I stood up to find a puddle of soft drink in my seat. I used more napkins to absorb the puddle.

As I sat back down and continued to try to absorb the soft drink with napkins, to my amazement, a quiet voice came from the back of my mind and said, "This is kind of cool and refreshing." Believe me, before using the techniques in this book that is *not* what I normally would have been thinking! Typically, I would have been upset at myself, angry, frustrated, and even furious. The negative self-talk in my head would have been thunderous.

As I listened to the quiet voice, I started to laugh. I knew the techniques were changing me for the better. My new unconscious response was much better than my old reaction would have been. Of course, the guy next to me didn't know that. As a result of my laughter he gave me the strangest look.

The plane arrived in Newark and I took a rental car for about an hour's drive to my hotel. I'm sure if I had been upset I would have gotten lost because of all the negative self-talk going on in my head.

The next morning, in preparing for my meeting, I realized the gray suit was the only one I'd brought, and it had a very large brown stain on the front of it. I remembered to use the Freeze-Frame technique as I noticed my anxiety rising. The answer I got was "make fun of it." So, as the accountants I was meeting with came into the room, I greeted each one and made a joke about the stain on my pants. They laughed, made a few polite jokes, and we had a very productive meeting. If I had not transformed my negative emotions by using the Freeze-Frame technique, I'm absolutely sure the outcome would not have been positive.

The point of the story is, even though we have tendencies or habits of negative emotional responses to certain situations, with regular use of the techniques we can change them into emotional responses that are much better for us.

What Can Happen When Two Executives Listen to Each Other

Len had reported to Randy through a variety of jobs as the two men had ascended the ladder to become executives in a large government agency. During the goal-setting interviews with each of them, I found out they didn't like each other all that much. In fact, because of their dislike for one another, their staffs hardly ever interacted, even though they worked in the same building. As it turned out, the two men were scheduled to attend our development program together.

Because I had 20 executives in the group, I didn't pay particular attention to the interaction, or lack of interaction, between Randy and Len. The format of this particular program included two days of training back-to-back, followed a week later by individual confidential coaching sessions, which were then followed two weeks later by a one-day group training session. Both men were making good progress in using the techniques they had learned during the initial two days of the program.

At the morning break on the third day, I noticed the two of them talking. I stopped and chatted with them for a moment. They interacted quite comfortably with each other as we talked. Then Randy said, "This program is really helping us." I asked him to explain. Len went on to say it was changing the way they interacted. In fact, they were now talking with each other and listening to each other on a daily basis. Randy explained that each of them had invited the other and his staff to attend their own staff meetings. They were already beginning to see the positive impact of the interaction out on the shop floor. Their staffs were coming up with new ideas to work together to improve the operation. The second coaching session and the impact interviews conducted with them two months later verified the improvements were continuing.

The point of the story is, long-held feelings of distrust, defensiveness, and pessimism toward another person can be transformed into an open, flexible, productive relationship with use of the techniques. If both people use the techniques, the positive change can be accelerated.

Even the Best-of-the-Best Sales People Can Improve

Before the development program began, Dick was a regional sales manager. Shortly after the program ended, he was promoted to the global accounts sales team. This team is responsible for taking away their competitors' largest customers. They are the cream of the crop, the best-of-the-best salespeople in this company. In the goal-setting interview with Dick, I learned he easily became angry with both customers and internal support people.

> **Internal associates, customers, and even his wife had started noticing the change in his behavior — a desirable change.**

During follow-up coaching sessions, it was obvious Dick was making good progress using the techniques. Internal associates, customers, and even his wife had started noticing the change in his behavior — a desirable change. Instead of getting frustrated with questions and walking away, Dick was starting to listen and value their points-of-view. They were no longer afraid to come and ask questions. Instead of being the first one to speak and then trying to convince people around his ideas, he was getting others to come up with ideas. This was giving them confidence and improving his own. Instead of multitasking when someone came to him with a problem, Dick stopped and gave them his full attention. He realized when he understood their point-of-view; it increased their motivation and helped them perform.

Dick was changing at home, too. Even though he had taken on a new job that required significantly more travel, he was taking time to dramatically improve the quality of time he had with his family. When he knew he was going to be out of town for part of the week, he even cooked the family dinner and made babysitter reservations so his wife could exercise in the evening.

Two and a half months after the development program, I asked Dick in his impact interview, "What would you tell other people about the program?" Dick said, "I'll do you one better than that; I'll tell you what I told my boss and the people on our team. We had a Global Accounts team meeting last month. Our boss told us to bring a "golden nugget" to the meeting to share about how we could each be a better global account manager. I told them about this program.

"We are the best-of-the-best. We live in a work world where we jump from one thing to the next. The emotions that can come into play can keep us from being effective. The techniques in the program help build relationships and nurture sales people so it doesn't affect them like it used to. These techniques can help us manage our stress and our jobs better. Emotions play a part in everything. Some things I was good at. But when I see the marked improvement, and others notice it, I see I was not as good at it as I thought."

> **Even hard-charging people who are high achievers benefit when they learn to manage their emotions and use techniques to demonstrate their empathy.**

The point of the story is, even hard-charging people who are high achievers in terms of their goals and professional accomplishments benefit when they learn to manage their emotions and use the techniques to demonstrate their empathy. Because of their passion and energy and the changes they personally experience, they often become proponents for the program and techniques.

Changes in the Boss Impact His Staff

LeRoy is an executive with a large government agency. During our impact interview two months after his training, it was obvious he was using all of the techniques frequently and was experiencing significant benefits himself. I asked him if he had noticed any change among his staff because of his own use of the techniques.

Two days earlier, LeRoy had held a staff meeting. After finishing everything on the agenda, he thanked his staff, but they didn't leave. He asked them if there was something they wanted to talk about, and they said there was. They told him about

> **"My staff has seen so much change in me as a result of my using the techniques, they now have the courage to speak up with their ideas."**

some problems encountered in a process he made them put in place a year earlier.

The bottom line was, 200 different locations were spending two hours a week using the process he mandated. His staff told him the process was not working well, and was not delivering the information needed in a timely fashion. He asked if they had any suggestions, which they did. He listened, asked questions, and then told them to implement their ideas.

The new process took only five minutes, could be done over the Internet, and was much more accurate and timely. I said, "LeRoy, your staff just saved 400 hours a week. I don't understand how this story relates to *your* use of the techniques." He said, "My staff has seen so much change in me as a result of my using the techniques in the program, they now have the courage to speak up with their ideas. They're not intimidated by my behavior, and I'm getting all kinds of cooperation and new ideas from them."

The point of the story is, people are more willing to offer ideas for improvement and innovation to a supervisor when they feel the supervisor will listen and will respond professionally. Supervisors and leaders who are not emotionally self-managed discourage participation, improvement, innovation, and destroy trust by their undesirable emotional behavior.

CLIENTS' COMMENTS FOR EACH TECHNIQUE

Reading these comments is optional, depending on the time you feel you can invest in reinforcing your dedication to using the techniques and sharpening your Emotional Intelligence skills.

The following pages offer a sampling of the thousands of comments received from participants two to three months after attending the development program. These comments were collected during face-to-face or telephone interviews. Participants were told ahead of time that while anonymity would be maintained, these comments were not confidential and would be shared with upper management and others. The comments are organized by technique.

#1 — "What Am I Feeling Right Now?"

- I've had a 20% improvement. There's no doubt I'm better than before because of this program. I stop to think about what I'm feeling. I think I still have a lot of opportunity for growth.
- I'm actually using this more. I used to be on autopilot all day and didn't pay attention to this. And yet, it affects decisions you make. I use it two to three times per day. Once you start to do it, it becomes automatic. You just start noticing. This makes it easier.
- I'm much more comfortable — knowing what I feel and not worrying about it. I confront difficulties. I'm vulnerable with people. People ask what I have done. I'm being more myself — not simply being "corporately compliant."
- This is the easiest one for me. I've gotten into the habit of stopping and thinking. It helps with the negative emotions and positive ones. I started with the negatives to catch them. Now I think of the positives and I'm having fun — like with my child's swim meet. You can get lost in the petty things instead of the important things.

> "I used to be on autopilot all day and didn't pay attention to this. And yet, it affects decisions you make."

- I'm really trying to put more specific words to how I feel and I'm being more honest with myself. It's helpful to get a better inventory.
- I'm much more aware of where the other person is trying to take things, instead of my trying to decide. As a result, I see improved alignment with several officers — those who had challenged me about what was holding me back from getting a higher position. What has come out of these discussions is increased alignment about how they can get to where they want to be — through their approach, not my approach. I'm much less frustrated. This is helping me turn off my switch and turn on theirs so I

can connect with them. This approach has taken anxiety out of me and has left me with more of a feeling of time. I'm getting my agenda done through other people.

#2 — Freeze-Frame Technique

- I use this daily several times — four to five times. I definitely use it when going between different challenges, like negotiating or a presentation with my boss. I use it to make changes to get in a positive frame of mind. It helps me let go of one meeting to be focused on the next. I'm becoming unconsciously competent. For example, in a negotiating session I was challenged. I would have cut this person off to get closure, but I let it go and took 10 minutes to get the situation right. I calmed down and figured out how to align positions better. I slowed down using the Freeze-Frame technique and moved forward with no raised voice and no upset emotions.

> "It helps me let go of one meeting to be focused on the next."

- I've had a 20-30% improvement in using it. I'm doing it before phone calls and one-to-one situations. I did the follow-up coaching with a peer and found it helpful. When it becomes part of a culture, it becomes a self-fulfilling prophecy. Our group is more highly interactive. There's more acceptance, more use, more risk-taking.

- I use it two to three times per day, purposefully — usually before meetings. It's not a big deal to do it. I use it almost without thinking about it. Sometimes I duck into a room to use it before a meeting. I'd rather be late to the meeting and be better focused. It helps me clear my head of the previous meeting. My meetings are more effective because I now have a goal in mind. I'm not as reactive — more purposeful.

> "Sometimes I duck into a room to use it before a meeting. I'd rather be late to the meeting and be better focused. It helps me clear my head of the previous meeting."

- I'm the subject matter expert on a particular product that was developed here. I got a call from a director who wanted to use another program. I was irritated. "I don't think that is a good idea," I said. This was a bad thing to say! She left my office. Then I used the Freeze-Frame technique, went to her office, and explained why using the external product wasn't a good idea. The results were good. The issue was resolved very well. She was quite happy and said we needed a mechanism to let people know that we have available a new process for greater efficiency. Had I not used the technique, I would have been angry and sent off an angry email to my boss. Instead, we had a good outcome from this interaction. This saves huge money and time.

- It's the most useful technique. I can tune in when my mind starts to degrade the situation and use the Freeze-Frame technique to put my mind and heart back into a positive atmosphere. The rewards are tremendous!
- I try to use it all the time with the kids when they're getting on my nerves. I take stock of where I'm at and put myself in a better place. When my child gets emotional, I have shown her how to use the Freeze-Frame technique. This has helped her a lot. I've seen dramatic changes in her. I'm using the software with the kids and even with neighborhood kids.
- I do it five or six times a day, depending on situations. It's the most effective way of making better decisions. The Heart Lock-In technique is good and helps you settle down, but the Freeze-Frame technique is very valuable too.

#3 — Appreciation

- Giving and receiving appreciation on the team builds trust. It motivates me to keep working. It lets me be more open to receive corrective feedback better because we have built trust.

> "I demonstrate appreciation back to myself too. It helps pull me out of doldrums. It keeps me from spiraling or sinking down."

- I've definitely increased this. In fact, it resonates and reminds me of the other techniques like Intuitive Listening. I use it daily. And I demonstrate appreciation back to myself too. It helps pull me out of the doldrums. It keeps me from spiraling or sinking down. It helps me not to be so hard on myself.
- I do it in multiple ways and shapes without question, daily. I look for times to recognize people. I try to recognize in a way that matches their experience and aligns with their work. There is a woman doing a lot of work for me. I talked to her as we were walking to a meeting and found that she and her family were going to a theme park on vacation. I called the theme park and gave her $100 in theme park dollars. So I tied my appreciation to something in her life to thank her for her work. I pay more attention to deeper conversations with folks so I can get to a high level of appreciation.
- We have a situation where a person is working very hard and long hours. The results are not very good yet because it will take time for the results to show up. I have really been showing appreciation to her because she is working so hard. I think the appreciation has opened up our communications even more. She feels that she can say whatever she wants to me — she does not feel that I don't care or won't listen.
- I use it at least every time my son brings something home from school, a couple of times a week. It's had a great impact on my

> "It's had a great impact on my relationship with my son."

relationship with my son.
- People have noticed an improvement. I was poor at it. I'm taking the opportunity to do it casually when I walk around and talk to my people. I catch myself more and spend more time listening in on the buzz with my staff. I would have never done this before. I would have been rushing.
- I actually do it more frequently now than at the end of the training program. As we approach deadlines, the pressure builds, and this is helpful to show my people how much I value them.
- I've done a 180° on this. I do it a lot. I feel better as a person. I have a vibrant team. They're more open with me, and this builds confidence and collaboration. I've had some feedback about my showing appreciation, and they really appreciate it. I had two team members whose relationship wasn't good with me. We have a far better relationship now. I attribute it to appreciation.

#4 — Heart Lock-In Technique

- I use this every day. It's my favorite thing. My heart rate is more stable. I notice it when it goes up. I get a feeling of relief when I'm done. I have more energy and a lot more creativity. I'm not stymied and I'm more open and freethinking. I can get there immediately. I sleep more deeply.

> "I get a feeling of relief when I'm done. I have more energy and a lot more creativity."

- We're faced with the need for productivity gains we need in the department. I met with work team leaders. I talked about strategy and team structure. I brought the corporate values with me and talked about them first. I used them to set the tone since they don't know the Freeze-Frame technique yet. I used the Heart Lock-In technique myself before the meeting to get my heart to dominate the tone of the meeting. Even though we had goals to accomplish, I wanted to have the human element involved — remind people to think about the people not just the roles/jobs — think about the people and not boxes with names.

> "Sleep has improved dramatically. I'm more rested and focused."

- I'm doing these almost every night. Sleep has improved dramatically. I'm more rested and focused.
- I use this four to five times a week. It's on my calendar at 8:15 at work. I come in 15 minutes early to do it. The impact is that physically and mentally I don't feel stressed any more over situations. I used to get stressed over driving to work and then be stressed at work. Now when I use the Heart Lock-In technique first thing at work, I can focus immediately on work instead of having my stress from driving spill over into my day.

- I use this every night before bed and periodically during the day. When meeting with team members, I'll use this even more frequently. I'm still sleeping better. I'm sleeping well, which I normally would not have. This is definitely helping me. I only do it when I need it at work or on the way home. I use the "Heart Zones" music. (See "Music and the Heart Lock-In technique," Chapter 3.)
- We used the Heart Lock-In technique in our group yesterday. The team is using it and they want to make sure we are using it regularly as a part of getting to hear each other and getting us focused.
- I'm finding that I do it throughout the day. When I have five minutes because a meeting ended early, I use the Heart Lock-In technique.

> "The glass is more 'half full' than 'half empty.' This makes me more upbeat."

- I use this four or five times a week. I'm more positive. I focus on the things that are going right. I do this much more frequently than I did before the training. The glass is more "half full" than "half empty." This makes me more upbeat.

#5 — Intuitive Listening

- I use this in every meeting I have. Most of the time I wait until a person finishes before I respond. I typically have three conference calls, plus four face-to-face meetings. I use this at least ten times a day. For example, I used it during a meeting with my boss and a colleague last Tuesday. We were creating an agenda for an important meeting. We created one and explained it to the boss. He listened, then responded by saying he had a different opinion on how to begin the meeting. My colleague and I fully listened to him. We used Intuitive Listening and realized we had missed something huge. We weren't defensive. The outcome was we had an excellent agenda. It saved time, great efficiency.
- This is fun. I was good at it before, but have gotten better. I have a situation where Engineering and Manufacturing do not see eye-to-eye. I listened to them and got to a

> "This helped me change to the person I want to be. I feel more in balance and whole."

good place and where to go next. A person in Engineering said, "I saw something interesting. You played the role of sitting back and not trying to drive it and you listened well to all comments and added clarification in context of what was going on and guided it passively using Intuitive Listening." I took this as a compliment. Using Intuitive Listening is my preferred way to deal with it — help them come to their own conclusion. It's better than dictating and helps get buy-in.
- It's one of my better disciplines. I thought I had strength in listening, now it's even stronger. I check my emotions at the door, especially with upper

management. I would have gone in thinking about how to persuade. Now I become a sponge and soak up to figure out how to approach them. I truly listen.

- I've used it during difficult discussions about organization structure changes. I used to jump in. Now I'm conscious of making sure I understand people. This course was brand new for me. The rest of the company's leadership development curriculum was basically reinforcement of what I knew. This helped me change to the person I want to be. I feel more in balance and whole. I felt the need to behave differently to be a better person. I find more meaning in the people side of the business now. Now the challenge that I'm enjoying and is invigorating me is making progress with the people-side of the business. It's a completely different set of skills than the ones that got me to my current position.

> "I find more meaning in the people-side of the business now."

CLIENTS' COMMENTS FOR EACH PERSONAL GOAL

On the following pages are listed a sampling of the thousands of comments received from clients two to three months after attending the development program. Participants were told ahead of time that while anonymity would be maintained, these comments were not confidential and would be shared with upper management and others. These comments are organized under each Personal Goal.

Goal #1 — Manage Emotional Reactiveness
- Last week I received an email from one of my employees about something that's probably one of the most emotionally difficult things any manager has to deal with. It hit me like a ton of bricks — completely unexpected. I felt like I had been kicked in the stomach. I felt ill and actually was sweating. I had to explain this to a number of people in Human Resources; reliving the impact of it each time I told it to someone else. What was amazing to me was that, by the end of the day, I was dramatically different emotionally than I expected to be. Not only was I in a neutral place with the email, I was actually seeing the positives — that an employee felt so safe that she could send such an email to me. That night I even slept well! If I had not been practicing the techniques taught in the course and recalling and applying the concepts and principles I learned, I would have been a nervous wreck and probably would not have gotten much accomplished that day or for several days after that. The situation is not resolved, but I'm confident that I'll handle it professionally and not let negative emotions get in my way of doing the best I can to resolve this positively.
- There was a meeting where I had to provide a review to Board members of a document. I was nervous. It was a very technical area. I managed my nervousness and calmed myself using the Freeze-Frame technique. I asked myself, "What will help me be more successful?" This helped. I felt good when it was done. I've done this before and have been worked up about it. My take-away was that it was a less painful way for me. In the past, I would have been worked up the night before. I didn't have to go through the rough, painful process.
- My problem is that I always react to things too fast. I'm very quick with a response. Any technique that causes me to pause is very good for me. I can edit myself if I pause. The Freeze-Frame technique has had a substantial impact on helping me do this.
- This is huge. With one leader in our company, I use the Freeze-Frame technique to prepare more, and we are meeting more often. I'm giving him the kind of information he wants and this has overcome his distrust and

suspicion. He is much happier, but is still demanding. I'm less frustrated. We are drawing him into our work so he doesn't shoot arrows at us. He has empathy now for what we go through. We now explain the detail, and he now understands.

Goal #2 — Reduce Stress and Worry

- I'm not as tired and have more energy for taking on bigger tasks during the day. I'm being more present in meetings with coworkers and clients. This probably has contributed to the reduction and almost elimination in migraine headaches.

> "My heart rate is down, I'm sleeping better, and my blood pressure is good. I feel the best I have in six months from an anxiety standpoint."

- My heart rate is down, I'm sleeping better, and my blood pressure is good. Since Christmas, I feel the best I have in six months from an anxiety standpoint.
- I've been so busy I haven't been able to exercise. I used what I learned about recognizing and managing emotions to the extent that I haven't had to run. I've survived and maintained peak performance without my normal outlet of daily exercise for a month. My level of frustration about no exercise is less too. I've kept on top of everything without freaking out.
- Being able to change what I'm feeling in-the-moment is helpful. It helped me get through my spouse's hospitalization.
- I'm a lot less stressed than before. I use the Heart Lock-In technique to get back to sleep. I still wake up thinking about work. But I don't stay awake for hours and then be dead tired going to work. This is probably the biggest benefit.
- One of the major roadblocks in being successful is that people are so busy and stretched. Stress comes along with that. I think I'm not the exception — everyone has to deal with it. When everyone is stressed and is not dealing with it well,

> "This program has changed my attitude— work hasn't changed, I have."

it's easy for situations to explode and make it hard to work personally and as a team. The program has helped me compartmentalize my free time so I don't think about work at home.
- I've had significant improvement here. I've had decreased sleeplessness, and, in general, less worry. I've had a general negative attitude around having way too much work to do and the stress of keeping up. Now I'm just getting that under control and saying, "It's O.K. Do what you can. I always figure it out." This program has changed my attitude — work hasn't changed, I have.

- I held things in and stewed over it before. Now I don't. My spouse made a comment. She noticed the change in me. I didn't tell her about this class. She said I had changed, "You're calmer." Then I told her about the class.

Goal #3 — Gain Greater Mental Clarity
- Using the Freeze-Frame technique allows me to go beyond and think outside the box. I was willing to go deeper. The customer was happy, and I was confident.
- I'm making better decisions, maybe not faster ones. I'm more thoughtful about more things — other people, teams, the company — but better decisions definitely. This is one of the best classes I've had. It depends on how much you take from it.
- I'm trusting my intuition much more than before. I'm able to be confident. My staff and I have designed processes together before and we would be argumentative and judgmental. Now we don't judge. It's a free form and very creative way to nail it on the head to go further than you ever did before. We get more clarity and are going deeper than before.
- The Freeze-Frame technique is the most obvious improvement. I'm using it before, during, and after various meetings and events. A lot of times, I use it before an event, but if I forget, I use it during — on the way in the room. I'm able to go from gut feeling to clearly being able to articulate a problem. I'm also trusting my intuition. I have more clarity to the intuition.

> "When stressed out, I'm able to calm down and clear my mind and be more productive."

- In Customer Service, we get seething emails and phone calls from customers. Now I wait. I look at it clearly by using the Freeze-Frame technique and make good, quick decisions rather than a bad decision or no decision. It's important to make good and fast decisions.
- I have more balance to my decision-making. I'm getting better input about it from people because I listen to and encourage them.
- I use the techniques to process data and listen to others. People feel better about the decisions I make, and I make more effective decisions. People are inclined to work with me on it.
- I'm doing a better job of letting others speak. It gives me a chance to hear where they're at and then drive forward.
- My improvement comes from stopping and reflecting — I think before reacting more. When stressed out, I'm able to calm down and clear my mind and be more productive.
- I'm a lot better. The program has taught me to take a time-out. Before I didn't think I could. Now I know it's OK to reflect rather than jump off the cliff.

Goal #4 — Increase Personal Productivity

- I start and end meetings on time. Intuitive Listening creates efficiencies. Last week in a training exercise, I was on a team that was very focused. We scored higher than any other team because I used the Freeze-Frame technique and Intuitive Listening and didn't allow emotions to get in the way.
- We had huge volume in August and September. I've been able to chip away at it. I've kept up with the increased volume with no increase in back log by using the techniques.
- Knowing what NOT to do has been big for me.
- Because there are so many activities to be done, using the Freeze-Frame technique or Neutral allowed me to delegate more appropriately. Example: Our Chart of Work — my role as the leader was not to do it myself, but to select leads for major portions. Before, I would have tried to work on all of them myself. Now I organize my work appropriately. I'm also using it to prioritize my work — one bite at a time. I don't get overwhelmed. This is huge for me. I ask, "What should I delegate?" during Step 4 of the Freeze-Frame technique.
- I've seen improvement. I was very productive before this class. When using the techniques like Intuitive Listening or the Freeze-Frame technique, I can be here more in-the-moment instead of having 100 things going on in my head. I've been able to improve productivity in a much shorter period of time.

> "I can be here more in-the-moment instead of having 100 things going on in my head."

- I'm doing a much better job in terms of personal productivity. I'm getting the little priorities down on paper and not making rushed decisions as to when I have to get to them. I'm not committing to a date and over-extending myself. I either need to talk to the person I committed to or delegate to my staff.
- I'm more focused. Instead of getting halfway done and reacting to something that pops up, I can better prioritize things. I used to just jump to the most noise.
- I was rubbish at it. There is an improvement. I have to say to you I'm more balanced in my life now. I used to think about the company 24 hours a day. They get less of my time outside of work now, but I have more balance and I'm more productive as a result of the balance. I can get even more productive.
- I'm being more focused. I get one task done before moving onto the next. The program really helped me here.

> "I see problems more as opportunities. I have more energy to solve problems."

Goal #5 — Stay Motivated In Spite of People or Events

- Our team of six went through your training together. My whole team is using these techniques individually and during interactions with each other. The result is that we listen to each other. We feel appreciated. Get more done. We start and end meetings on time. We get more creative solutions to problems. Work is fun for me, and I look forward to coming to work every day.
- I have a more positive attitude. I'm looking at the things that are going well. This energizes me to look at the things that aren't. I see problems more as opportunities. I have more energy to solve problems.
- Personal motivation is dramatic. Getting my life back is dramatic. Some things I've done that I wouldn't have done before this program.
- Using what I've learned has helped me see different options in difficult situations and stay motivated about things over which I have no control.
- It feels pretty good to me. There is a big up-tick in high priority issues. I've been able to recognize what I can't influence, or influence yet, and not worry about it. It's helping me focus. So I'm not going to worry about something that is not here right now.
- I've experienced improvement just from the standpoint of being able to use the Freeze-Frame technique and get myself squared away. With Appreciation and showing it and using Intuitive Listening I have a more positive outlook. I feel good when I give appreciation and can see the impact.
- My boss can be frustrating. He is not going to change. He is going to "blow-up" every once in a while so I don't get upset now. I roll through it. I appreciate him for what he does for me.
- I have clarity in direction and in how to implement things in context of the bigger picture. I'm ahead of the wave.
- I'm not getting frustrated about how the company is moving forward. I'm not letting it bring me down. I can handle it better. I'm more motivated than I was before.

> "Using what I've learned has helped me see different options in difficult situations and stay motivated about things over which I have no control."

- I'm having a more positive attitude about coming to work. This ties into less stress and more confidence that I'll figure things out. It helps me stay motivated.

Goal #6 — Develop More Self-Confidence

- I have a greater understanding of what I have to contribute. During the review of a project with the steering team, one team member was trying to take credit. In a good way, I made sure it was known who initiated it and

who should get credit without upsetting the person who was trying to take credit. My intent is to build better relationships between departments and get away from the "throw-it-over-the-wall" approach to problems.
- I have more self-confidence, especially in large groups. I used to just sit back and not say anything and get nervous or uncomfortable. Now I use the Freeze-Frame technique and have experienced 100% improvement from the way I was. I'm not nervous like before. I tend to say things more slowly so people can understand. There's so much more clarity in what I say.
- My confidence in my success in communicating my ideas has increased significantly. I've become more skilled in selling concepts/ideas to my boss and my boss's boss. The senior leaders pick up these ideas, think they're their ideas, and are running with them. Before I would have tried more to take credit for ideas; now I just want to be helpful and I care less about the 'credit.'
- I've been much more conscious in the way I pitch something; more thoughtful about how others will respond to it. In the past, in a meeting full of people, I might be critical of the strategy or approach a person is using. Now I talk with them one-on-one so they won't feel defensive. And during these conversations, having greater empathy about their potential emotional reaction helps me present alternatives that they more readily embrace.

> **"I've become more skilled in selling concepts or ideas to my boss and my boss's boss."**

- I've been much better at dealing with other people and allowing them to feel confident about me. I tended to be the first one to speak and then convince others around my idea. Now in teams, when coming up with a strategy, I get others to come up with ideas. I don't shoot them down. I find out why their issue or idea is good — this gives others confidence and I'm confident in them too.
- I will now speak up on behalf of other people. I'm more people oriented. I used to be brutal. Now I speak up for the people. I took out 15% of all temporary work force before Christmas. I was told by headquarters to take out 20% more. I said, "No." This was too much risk for the business and not the right thing to do for people. I'm not just doing what upper levels want to hear. Taking out additional people would have sent shock waves across the business.

Goal #7 — Increase Personal Creativity
- I now have techniques in my toolbox to not stymie my thinking. I have freedom to let loose of everything and go to deep creativity in my brain and heart. I've gotten pretty creative on how to do protocols. I could be absorbed and obsessed, but by managing my team more effectively, we hit a home run.

- Through Intuitive Listening, I'm helping others create alternatives instead of digging their heels in to defend their ideas. For example, I was asked to help resolve a problem in a team. A project had stalled, and there were different groups here and outside of the U.S. blaming each other for lack of progress. In the meeting I was asked to become involved. In explaining the situation to me in the meeting, this person's explanation made no sense to me. I didn't blame him/her for my lack of understanding or embarrass him/her. With the Freeze-Frame technique, I was more careful about how I reacted. Later I spoke to people one-on-one outside of the meeting environment. I listened to various points-of-view, using Intuitive Listening. I then played back to everybody what I thought I heard them say and suggested the steps needed to move forward. Later two people came forward independently and thanked me for moving the project forward. The thing was, I knew nothing about the project and was asked only two days ago to try to get it moving. I got people energized and working together to achieve their team's goals. Before the class, there would have been a temptation to try to solve the problem then and there in the meeting by telling the guy he didn't make sense and that he was the problem. Instead, I recognized that the meeting environment wasn't the ideal forum to get to the bottom of the problem. I wasn't going to alienate the working relationships. People would have dug into their trenches; the project would have stalled until it got to the senior management level to fix it. Organizationally, we saved time and money.
- I'm trying to be creative with my team. They ask for things, and I come up with ideas to help them when I can't give them what they need. Win-win situations have gotten "thumbs up" responses from my team. I want to have it continue and be more often.
- With my being calmer and more cognizant of my feelings, I found that I'm able to come up with unique new possibilities to projects and problems — I can hear above the din. Now I can stop, feel, think and come up with ideas. Neutral and the Heart Lock-In technique have helped me slow down and better clarify my thoughts. There's not as much worry banging around in my head.
- We are working on a project anticipating problems with a new corporate initiative. We're recommending solutions in advance to solve them. In the process, the tendency is to go to obvious solutions. Using the techniques has enabled me to come up with far more creative solutions and not just understand but to also embrace the initiative. I'm thinking of things from a new perspective — not just facts, but also the emotional appeal to things.

Goal #8 — Increase Change Flexibility
- Resiliency has changed things from "the flavor-of-the-day" to a listening point, especially with my boss. My boss fires without adequate

knowledge. He shoots from the hip, and I saw him wrecking my day. Now I listen for the good point, wait for my boss to come back in a few days and be clearer. I'm more flexible in the face of change. I used to do the same with my own team. This has helped me talk with my team so I don't do to them what my boss does to me. Now I don't rock their world.

> "This has helped me talk with my team so I don't do to them what my boss does to me. Now I don't rock their world."

- There have been a couple of occasions where my boss threw us a curve ball — different ideas or directions. Just by my being more aware of listening and not jumping in, I'm not disagreeing with him. I listen to others' positions and I do it in a way so that I understand where others are at.
- I've improved. I've taken on new assignments. My responsibilities will change again. I'm not upset about it. It doesn't really upset me — it's like "we will work through it" as opposed to "the sky is falling."
- I've had great improvements. I love change. I was good with change before, but with the techniques, it's much better. I used to try to push an idea too much. People got frustrated with my "in-your-face" style. Now I do emails that are more reasoned. I could come up with ideas before. Now I get more results by asking, "What do you think?"

> "I was good with change before, but with the techniques, it's much better."

- I think in pictures and I feel as though this program has added a concentric circle around me further out so I feel more comfortable with things around me. Personally, I've really been working on this. This is about risk-taking.
- Some of the things that have bothered me or that I over-cared about — some of that is not feeling as big. I'm feeling OK with it not being my responsibility. I feel better about things. I have techniques to help me. It makes a difference because it changes your perspective.
- Just working with this company you're used to change. I've improved on taking the change more easily and being less worried and concerned and frustrated with it. I have less fear than before. I react more positively.

Goal #9 — Increase Personal and Professional Balance

- I'm keeping work in perspective. Things feel more balanced. There is a huge list of things to be done, but instead of it being a problem or a drain, I see these things more as an opportunity. I leave problems at work. I'm not feeling overwhelmed. Before, at times, I got wrapped up with work, took it home and stewed on it, worrying about it.

- I'm able to keep work from affecting home and vice versa. I can move from one to the other. It's more quality than quantity. This is increasing my optimal ability to be happy in both.

> *"This is about being 'in-the-moment.' I used to be at home thinking about work. This program has allowed me to be at home and really be with my family."*

- This is about being "in-the-moment." I used to be at home thinking about work. This program has allowed me to be at home and really be with my family. I can focus on what I need to do. I can help my children. I now read my work stuff at work and not at home instead of halfway engaging with my family. I'm less guilty about separating the two parts of my life.
- This is going really well. I thought there would not have been improvement with the travel I do now. But the ability to take the time at home to improve the quality has been a dramatic improvement. I really listen to my wife and children and talk about issues and don't walk out. I'm using the Freeze-Frame technique too, before the day starts and when dealing with the kids. I help my spouse prepare even though I'm not there. I cook dinner on Sunday for the week if I'm going out of town. My spouse has commented about my doing this. I call babysitters for my spouse if I'll be out of town.

> *"My kids have seen me interact with them more. They have been asking about the change in me. Now they see me being more fun and laughing more."*

- Definitely, I've improved. It has helped me gain perspective about how things at work have negatively affected my life. I've recognized how stressed I was by things outside my control at work. The training highlighted this and allowed me to get some balance back.
- My kids have seen me interact with them more. They have been asking about the change in me. Now they see me being more fun and laughing more. My oldest child voiced that she liked the way we have dinner and share with each other now.
- I'm a lot more conscious of the need to draw the line between work and play. When I'm at home it's higher quality time. I used to work Sunday and think about work from 10:00 a.m. until going to bed. Now, if I notice work creeping in — unless it must get done — I give the time to my family. It helps with my balance.

Goal #10 — Understand Others
- Using Intuitive Listening, really listening for understanding is huge. People feel more valued. My biggest improvement is continuously using

the technique, building better dialogue and better relationships. I'm giving my counterpart the opportunity to really share his concerns.
- I have some regular meetings where I don't interrupt now. I've noticed that I would have cut them off and misunderstood them. I would have been incorrect in my thinking. I'm better listening, not prejudging them. The impact on them is they feel heard, less frustrated, not as upset. I'm able to get truer meaning of their perspective.
- I'm able to see it from their point-of-view rather than just charging forward. Example: I've said, "Just never thought of that before," more than I've ever said it before. This impacts others and me positively — they feel more valued, and we have more teamwork and more camaraderie.
- Intuitive Listening — I'm doing more of it. I get a better understanding of others. In the past, I would multi-task. I don't do that anymore. I'm not shy to ask for another time to give them my full attention. This has been huge for me. In the past people would avoid me because I was "me-focused." Those days are gone. When I understand what's going on with them, it helps them perform and want to perform better.

> "I'm not jumping to conclusions. I take time to listen. It's amazing what I was missing."

- This comes from recognizing that not everyone has the same goals or needs or targets as I have and asking, "How do we jointly improve or affect each other's measures."
- I'm slowing down with my spouse and people that work for me. I'm not jumping to conclusions. I take time to listen. It's amazing what I was missing.
- I always considered others' feelings, but would consider it after a decision. Now I consider their feelings before, so I get the better decisions.
- The Freeze-Frame technique helps here. By using Appreciation, I often understand other people's emotions and positions.

Goal #11 — Listen More, Talk Less
- By demonstrating my ability to listen and help others get their jobs done, I'm building trust and building relationships. As I sell ideas to the senior management team this way, it has built their trust in me. The reality is that people talk to those who can help solve their problems; people go to people they trust. I feel like I'm adding more value.
- I was good at this before the program. I do this more with family, when my spouse or kids share something, when my kids have joy. I don't want to diminish their joy by ignoring them or telling them not to do something, so I stop and enjoy their emotions. Now I realize how important it is to emotionally share their joy during those short 10-15 second encounters.

You can see the smile on their faces when they know you've connected with them on this. I'm more fully present for them.
- I'm feeling better about asking questions and letting people talk. I'm taking things at face value.
- I've had numerous occasions to listen more and talk less with an officer. In contract negotiations, he is the accountable person. He gave me direct feedback. I asked clarifying points which opened the door to talk about a difficult situation in Germany. In the end, I couldn't do much about it. I didn't react, but let it go awhile, and he took accountability for fixing it. Before this program, I would have put myself through anguish.
- I listen because people have different styles — adjusting to different styles is so important. I'm a "get down to business" person. Now I can take the time to listen and get my work done.
- Now I'm not lecturing, but slowly introducing my ideas and getting them to bite.

Goal #12 — Manage Relationships More Effectively

- In my leadership position here, I'm using the techniques and managing relationships better by being more careful and conscious of what I say and how I say it. I'm more aware of how others might take what I say. I use the Freeze-Frame technique and ask myself how this person is going to perceive what I say and do. I ask myself, "Is what I want to say going to enhance them and help them get their job done?" Before the class, I might have opened my mouth first and thought about their reaction too late. I would be too blunt for the environment I'm in. In the company I used to be in, people were able to be blunt about problems. Here in this environment, people are softer; we have to talk about opportunities, not problems. I'm better able to do this now.

> **"I can sense an openness in others to work with me because I'll listen to them."**

- This is one of my personal goals, and I'm making really good progress here. It's still early. I expect the percent to go up even further from 40% improvement in this Personal Goal. I can sense an openness in others to work with me because I'll listen to them.
- This is a real improvement for me. With account development managers it's important to stay in communication. I don't always give them the answer they want, but it's important to have a good relationship. I've been more deliberate about making sure our relationship is solid.
- Through changing my behavior and listening, this is a huge improvement. It's not that I disrespected them in the past. There is a behavior shift on my part.
- I'm now always able to listen better and find a compromise that is beneficial.

- Using Appreciation has been huge on this. This month had month end reporting. I worked on it together with another person. I thanked her for her help and what she did that was done well. I was targeting the appreciation so she keeps doing that — not that everything is done well yet. I found that it's important to show appreciation for people that are not your direct reports. It almost means more coming from someone not in their own department.
- My relationships benefit due to listening and understanding and working together rather than someone telling me what to do all the time. Intuitive Listening opens doors.
- I'm not jumping in — not doing "ready, shoot, aim." My tone is better even in a positive situation.

> "In the past, my approach was to try to influence through my knowledge or technical expertise. Now I influence by listening to other's issues."

Goal #13 — Influence Others

- I have greater sensitivity to what the business problems are that another person wants solved. Before, my strategy was, "How can I promote my ideas and myself?" Now the way I would do that is to give those ideas away by helping someone else get their job done, help them look good, and achieve results they can own.
- The biggest example is working with a VP on IT warehousing strategy. This is my responsibility, but officers think I'm jaded in my thinking because I want measurement and analysis. One of the executives should take the lead in putting together a more comprehensive strategy. I was frustrated initially. She and I have differences of opinions. Once I learned and started using the Emotional Intelligence techniques, I've been much calmer about the process. I have stepped back, thinking there must be a reason why they chose this person. The executives will feel accountability because ideas are coming from one of their peers instead of me. This has worked out tremendously. I let someone else drive it.
- I'm taking a different approach. In the past, my approach was to try to influence through my knowledge or technical expertise. Now I influence by listening to other's issues.

> "I'm not jumping in—not doing 'ready, shoot, aim.' My tone is better even in a positive situation."

- This is subliminal. I'm not cutting people off. I'm using the Freeze-Frame technique ahead of time and have a full state of mind when I'm with others. I can use their emotions to help me modify my position, and use it to my advantage. I know their emotions before they do.
- I'm much more calm. When I get excited people appreciate it, but I talk at warp speed. I've already thought about it. I've slowed down with

information so they can get it. It has helped in them taking initiative and their confidence. I don't have to say it four to five times.
- The Freeze-Frame technique and Intuitive Listening are helping me learn how people think. They help me hear what others are not saying as much as what they are saying. They're helping me speak up in ways that bring people into alignment instead of fighting for different points-of-view. For example, in a conference call, a customer was selling a solution. Before, I wouldn't have spoken up when I disagree, but I said I had a question about how something was going to be presented. My boss then said she agreed with me. The boss then presented a new solution. I didn't think that would work either, so I again raised an objection by saying I was confused. Before, I would have disagreed more forcefully and created defensiveness. My boss saw my point-of-view and said, "Let's change it." In other words, I had influenced him to change his mind on his own idea.

> "By not being as impatient, I avoid comments made in the heat of the moment. I avoid putting more fuel on the fire and avoid getting personal."

Goal #14 — Resolve/Manage Conflict

- I'm defusing it. Slowing down makes the difference. It's not about you or me. I work to get the focus off the person and on to the problem and project. People are trusting and following me more.
- I've improved both internally on the team and with my family members. I stop, use the Freeze-Frame technique, and see things more clearly. I listen and show empathy, which has reduced conflict within the team or reduced it and improved our ability to deal with it. It's not just what I did. My behaviors become part of the team dynamic. I'm the catalyst. I get them headed down the right path. The whole thing circles back to morale and motivation. I can be in a vicious cycle or virtuous cycle and it depends on me as the leader. The same thing applies at home.
- There is less conflict for me, or it feels like it's not conflict because I'm not stressed out, not in turmoil. We may not agree more, but it's easier to accept different points-of-view.

> "I can be in a vicious cycle or virtuous cycle and it depends on me as the leader."

- I realize when the other person's emotions are starting to rise. Instead of getting trapped in that, I calm down, and they calm down. I saw this with my boss. He was upset. I was calm, listened, and let him blow. Then I was calm in giving input. It's amazing! He calms down to my level and apologizes — it becomes obvious. When it's all over, you're not regretting what you did. You know you did all you could instead of being vindictive so it doesn't feel uncomfortable in a meeting later.

- Regarding the 10K report — It was late in the game ready to go to the printer, and an officer asked for it to be reviewed by someone who is an incredibly detailed but not substantive reviewer. We didn't have time to deal with all the minor little subjective things she identified. If it were meaningful, we would have. I could feel my heart pounding and blood pressure rising. I used the Freeze-Frame technique. I let the person know I was interested in comments, but may not make her suggested changes. She kept wanting me to make the changes. I did a heavy-duty Freeze-Frame technique and it helped a tremendous amount. I was sold on the technique then and there. I could understand where she was coming from and found a better way to deal with it. It could have turned into an ugly situation. I felt that I didn't do something to regret and can talk to the person with no baggage. If I had gotten upset, it would have gotten back to the officer and would have given me a black eye.
- By not being as impatient, I avoid comments made in the heat of the moment. I avoid putting more fuel on the fire and avoid getting personal.

Goal #15 — Improve Morale/Motivation

- People are more willing to come up and talk to me. I have definitely improved, and people have commented about the positive change they see in me.
- In my team, we are looking at a 50% improvement in this goal. It helps that we all took the training together. There is no cause to expect that someone has a private agenda. We have a great deal of trust.
- Trust continues to grow. Intuitive Listening has helped. They know I'm not trying to run their show or strong-arm them.
- My boss has pooh-poohed a new executive. Instead of agreeing, I said, "Let's hope that, in a year, we can say this person has come a long way." I try to move things forward.
- I have to continue to be consistent over time. People are always looking to see if you revert. My previous tendency was to be personally critical of people and get highly critical. Now I think I might be able to help this person. I'm sensing people beginning to think I'm trying to be consciously different.
- In a meeting, people began complaining about and belittling a recent company decision. After listening to this for a minute, I asked the question, "I wonder how long we have to have this discussion before we've spent as much time and energy on it as the company has spent examining the issue so they could make a decision about it?" This was a polite way to say, "Stop crabbing about it." It felt like I had a powerful impact on people. If you have two buckets, gas and water, which will you pour on the fire?

- I'm trying to keep things balanced and not let specific situations or issues get too important. I keep the stress out of it and not let it go in a negative spiral.
- This is part of transparency, one of company values. As I left to come here, one of my people freaked out. I told him what I know about the situation that was bothering him. I was forthright, sharing information. People need to know that you care and pay attention to their world. I'm trying to be more open. I was accused in the past of not caring.

Goal #16 — Improve Teamwork

- Last year, on a project with a lot of players, I was driving it and excluding people from being really engaged. Now I carefully include them, and it definitely has built greater teamwork. I've listened to them more carefully and communicated greater appreciation for their contributions.

> "There is an ease of getting things done. I get people to buy in much more easily now. I don't stampede people like I used to."

- Too often, as managers, we get too far away from the battle. Spending time with team members to get them to understand the level of urgency and the crucial part their role is in the outcome is important. I ask them on a regular basis what they need to get their job done. I identified and knocked down the roadblocks. Initially, one of my people said she wasn't going to make the deadline on a project. But I removed the roadblocks for her and she did pull it out.
- It's working great. I can't compare improvement because we were a new team when we learned these techniques together. But we use these techniques all the time. There is a great deal of trust and full engagement.
- There is an ease of getting things done. I get people to buy in much more easily now. I don't stampede people like I used to.
- There have been inter-department work team issues — my team and other teams inside the department. There's been some unhappiness on both sides. I ask myself how I can make this more effective. I've explained Intuitive Listening to the team and have been demonstrating behavior to other people. It's been helping.
- Because I'm empathetic, I gain more trust of the people. They want to participate and cooperate.
- Because of less tension and stress caused by me, it helps my team work more effectively together.

Goal #17 — Improve Team-to-Team Cooperation/Coordination

- We get caught up in dynamics between different departments regarding the price increase in August. Decisions had to be made, and there was a lot of miscommunication. People were pissed and mad — coming to shoot us. I could have smooshed them with an email. I truly listened to them, Sales, and my people. The reality was that everyone was right. Instead of being defensive, I got all the people together to understand and not point fingers. Before, I would have shot first and talked to the living. It's different now. I smoothed and soothed and built relationships instead of tearing them down — we value them — this is huge.

> "Before, I would have shot first and talked to the living. It's different now. I smoothed and soothed and built relationships instead of tearing them down — we value them — this is huge."

- I've seen huge improvements in working through a project. I use the Freeze-Frame technique before the conversations and walk into it with a better attitude. It's a way of being in a different state of mind — not negative but positive or neutral. I'm building relationship before we get to those meetings and now having personal conversations we would never have had before. By showing appreciation to them it puts them in a mindset to help you next time — instead of complaining. We've gone from a tense, poor output to "teaming" on the situation, which is leading to better results.

- We're very efficient now. Without the training, our team would have been struggling with all the challenges we face. We have a diverse international team. Diversity is hard to manage. With the techniques, we recognize the benefits of working together.

> "Diversity is hard to manage. With the techniques, we recognize the benefits of working together."

- The team, including the new international team, experienced a 10-20% improvement in teamwork. Having the follow-up Peer Coaching helped. We spoke every week for a month, then every other week for two months. We inspired each other.

- We are still forming and will start working with other teams. The governance model we came up with using the techniques and the way we involved other teams made sure they had input. We established a collaborative environment, and I'm sure it will continue.

- I agreed to a change that a manager wanted us to make. When he talked with his people, he found out that there were so many other applications out there that would have to change, that they decided not to do it. So we have built up credit for the next time we want to do something. My willingness to change to help his team has built up a "bank account" with him and his team. If I had said, "No," they would have forced it through, though it's not the best thing for them or the company.

DATA

The following pages list sample results data collected from clients after attending development programs in which the techniques were taught. The title of the program varies based on the client organization's preferences, but the techniques taught are the same as the ones in this book.

Various Results Data
- High Potential Managers, Directors, and Vice-Presidents
- International IT Team
- Leaders and Managers — U.S. Government
- First Level Managers
- Creative Professionals
- Hypertension Study — High Tech Company

High Potential Managers, Directors, and Vice-Presidents
Multi-Billion-Dollar Company Reports Success

Sixty-three high-potential managers, directors, vice-presidents, and senior vice presidents of a multi-billion-dollar manufacturing company participated in our Developing Emotional Competence™ program.

The 63 participants were trained in four groups. Because of the success these four groups experienced, the program was offered to anyone in the company through their ongoing leadership curriculum. Two months after the final development session for each group, confidential one-hour interviews were conducted with a 49% sample of participants, to gauge program effectiveness. Participants were asked to share improvements they experienced in the Personal Goals for the program. Following are the average results reported for both the intra-personal and interpersonal goals.

As reported by Impact Interview participants, the frequency of use of a technique relates to the improvement in the two Personal Goals shown here: Influence Others, and Increase Personal Productivity. The dots on the graph indicate reports by individuals of frequency of use and percent improvement. Notice even with very modest use of a technique, once or twice a week, significant improvement is experienced by some participants. Others experience similar improvements from using the technique daily. In general, it is safe to say that for most people, the more frequently a technique is used, the greater the improvement.

CHAPTER 4 — RESULTS   163

Figure 31.
Average Improvements in Personal Goals

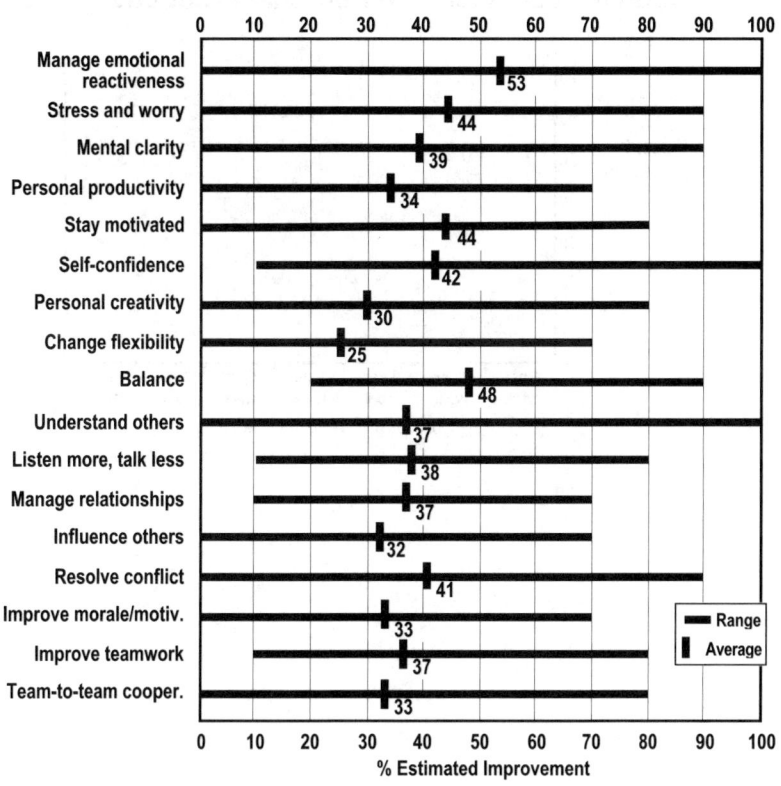

Personal Goal	Average %
Manage emotional reactiveness	53
Stress and worry	44
Mental clarity	39
Personal productivity	34
Stay motivated	44
Self-confidence	42
Personal creativity	30
Change flexibility	25
Balance	48
Understand others	37
Listen more, talk less	38
Manage relationships	37
Influence others	32
Resolve conflict	41
Improve morale/motiv.	33
Improve teamwork	37
Team-to-team cooper.	33

% Estimated Improvement

Source: Byron Stock & Associates

Figure 32.
Personal Goal: Influence Others

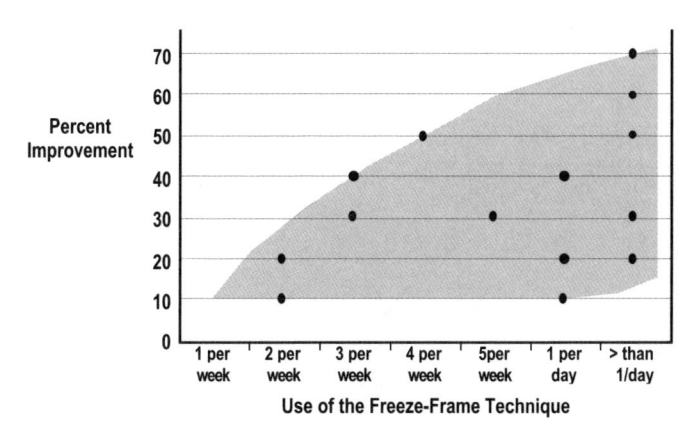

Use of the Freeze-Frame Technique

Source: Byron Stock & Associates

164 CHAPTER 4 — RESULTS

**Figure 33.
Personal Goal: Increase Personal Productivity**

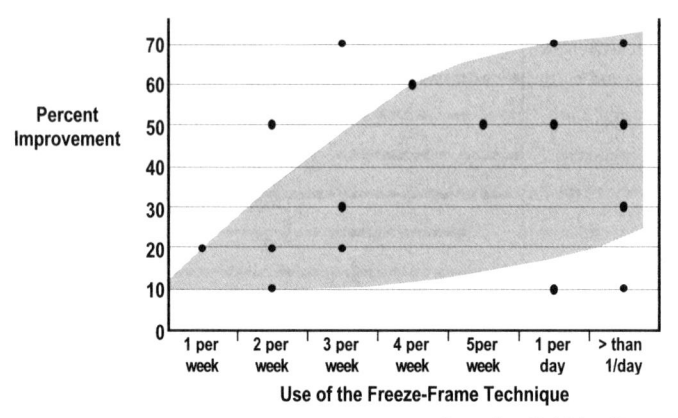

Source: Byron Stock & Associates

International IT Team
Focus: Managing Stress, Influencing Others

In early 2005, a newly formed international IT team of a global company participated in the Developing Emotional Competence™ program. The focus of the development program for this team was to enable them to manage stress more effectively and to influence international and corporate associates in developing and adopting new point-of-sale software.

Figure 34.
Personal Goals Improvements

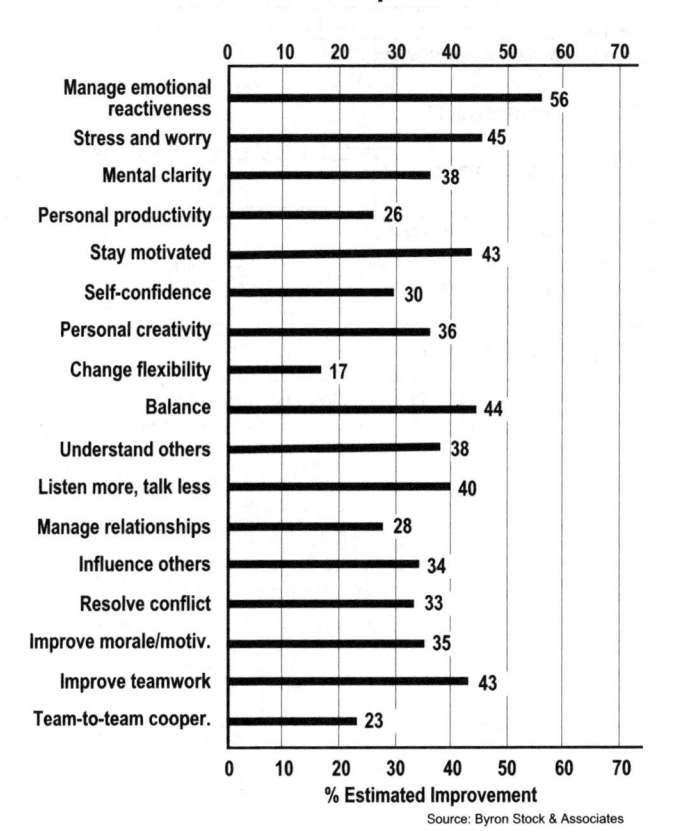

Personal Goal	% Estimated Improvement
Manage emotional reactiveness	56
Stress and worry	45
Mental clarity	38
Personal productivity	26
Stay motivated	43
Self-confidence	30
Personal creativity	36
Change flexibility	17
Balance	44
Understand others	38
Listen more, talk less	40
Manage relationships	28
Influence others	34
Resolve conflict	33
Improve morale/motiv.	35
Improve teamwork	43
Team-to-team cooper.	23

Source: Byron Stock & Associates

The 11 participants were trained in late January. Two months after the last development session, confidential, one-hour interviews were conducted with nine, or 82%, of the participants to gauge program effectiveness. Participants were asked to list improvements they experienced in the Personal Goals for the program. The average results reported for both the intrapersonal and interpersonal goals are shown above.

Leaders and Managers — U.S. Government
Results of a Survey Eight Months Post-Training

Over 120 leaders and managers in a large U.S. government organization participated in our Developing Emotional Intelligence Skills™ program. Eight months after the training a follow-up survey was sent to participants. It showed dramatic increases in key aspects of personal effectiveness.

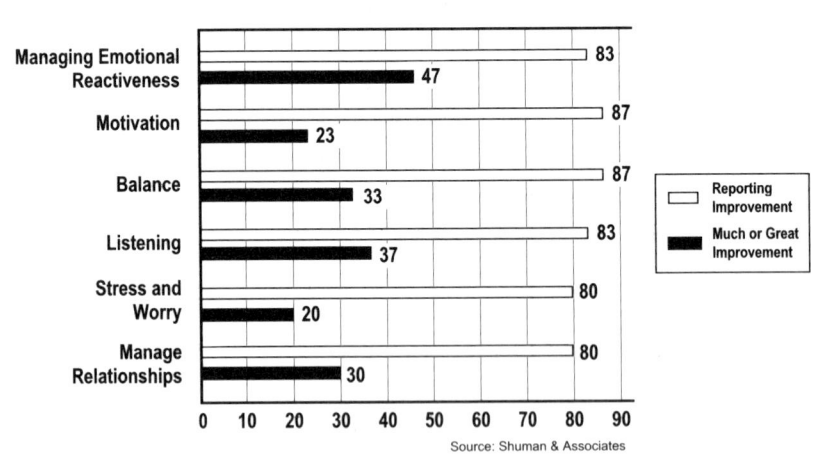

**Figure 35.
Improvements after 8 Months**

Category	Reporting Improvement	Much or Great Improvement
Managing Emotional Reactiveness	83	47
Motivation	87	23
Balance	87	33
Listening	83	37
Stress and Worry	80	20
Manage Relationships	80	30

Source: Shuman & Associates

New, First-Level Managers
Pre-and Post Data Show Dramatic Improvements

When two groups totaling 33 new, first-level managers completed the Enhancing Personal Effectiveness™ (EPE) program, pre-and post-data showed dramatic improvements in a number of factors (see Figures below) that contribute to improved productivity, quality, communication, creativity, and professional and personal balance.

Figure 36.
Reduced Symptoms of Stress

Symptom	Pre Training	Post Training
Anger	49	45***
Fatigue	52	46**
Anxiety	55	44*
Depression	47	42**
Sadness	49	41**
Distress	50	43*

* statistically significant at .05 level
** statistically significant at .01 level
*** statistically significant at .001 level

Source: Byron Stock & Associates

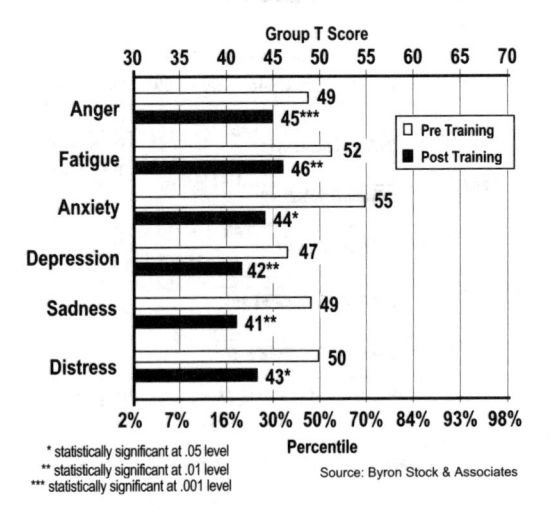

Figure 37.
Improved Effectiveness

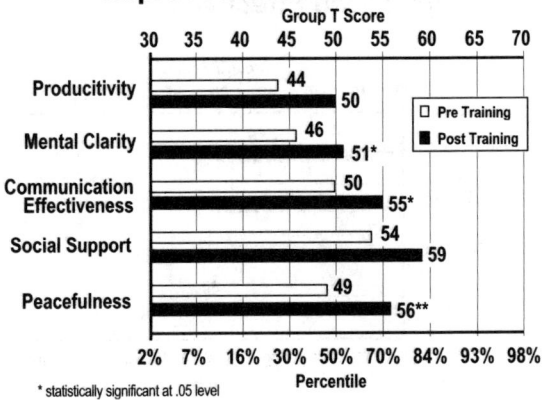

Factor	Pre Training	Post Training
Producitivity	44	50
Mental Clarity	46	51*
Communication Effectiveness	50	55*
Social Support	54	59
Peacefulness	49	56**

* statistically significant at .05 level
** statistically significant at .01 level

Source: Byron Stock & Associates

Creative Professionals
Assessment Survey Reveals Progress

A creative department of an international foods company completed the Developing Emotional Intelligence Skills program in the spring of 1998. Pre- and post-data from the Personal and Organizational Quality Assessment (POQA) survey instrument used to measure results of the program showed dramatic improvements in a number of factors. A portion of that data is presented below.

Figure 38.
Reduced Symptoms of Stress

Factor	Pre Training (Group T Score)	Post Training (Group T Score)
Anger	45	41
Depression	47	42*
Distress	46	39**
Rapid Heartbeats	53	45*
Indigestion	52	46

Percentile scale: 2%, 7%, 16%, 30%, 50%, 70%, 84%, 93%, 98%

* statistically significant at .05 level
** statistically significant at .01 level

Source: Byron Stock & Associates

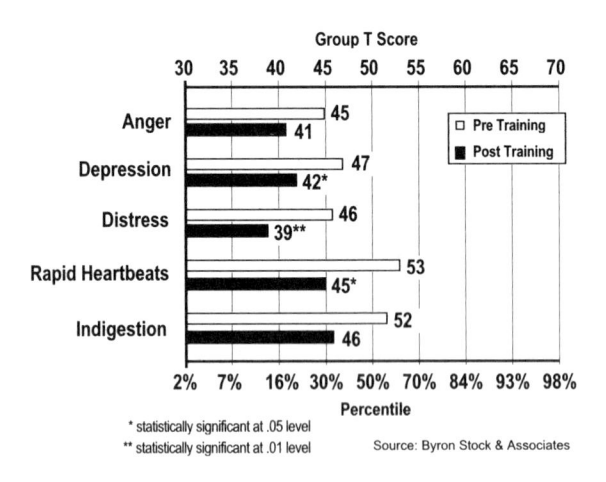

Figure 39.
Improved Effectiveness

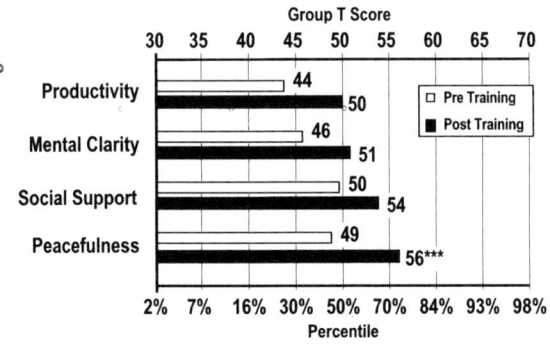

Factor	Pre Training (Group T Score)	Post Training (Group T Score)
Productivity	44	50
Mental Clarity	46	51
Social Support	50	54
Peacefulness	49	56***

Percentile scale: 2%, 7%, 16%, 30%, 50%, 70%, 84%, 93%, 98%

*** statistically significant at .001 level

Source: Byron Stock & Associates

Hi-Tech Company
Research Study of Hypertension and Emotional Management Skills

Thirty-eight hypertensive men and women from a Fortune 100 High Tech company participated in the study. Participants were divided into a randomized target group (to be trained first in the Inner Quality Management® program), and a "waiting control" group (which received the program later).

**Figure 40.
Improved Blood Pressures**

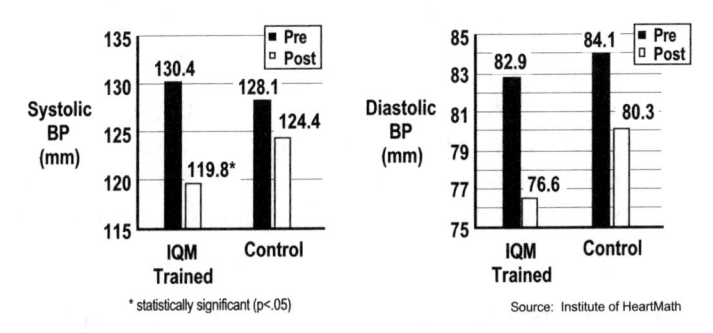

Systolic BP (mm): IQM Trained Pre 130.4, Post 119.8*; Control Pre 128.1, Post 124.4
Diastolic BP (mm): IQM Trained Pre 82.9, Post 76.6; Control Pre 84.1, Post 80.3

*statistically significant (p<.05)

Source: Institute of HeartMath

A statistically significant reduction in systolic blood pressure, from 130.4 to 119.8 mm, was shown over a three-month period among people who were trained to use the same techniques as those in this book.

In addition to reducing blood pressure, numerous significant improvements in key indicators of both personal and organizational effectiveness were reported. Dramatic, simultaneous improvements were shown in employee attitudes, performance, and health. Significant improvement in Value of Contribution was seen in the trained participants, compared to almost no change among the control group.

Inner Quality Management is a registered trademark of the Institute of HeartMath.

Figure 41.
Improved Attitudes: Value of Contribution, Job Satisfaction

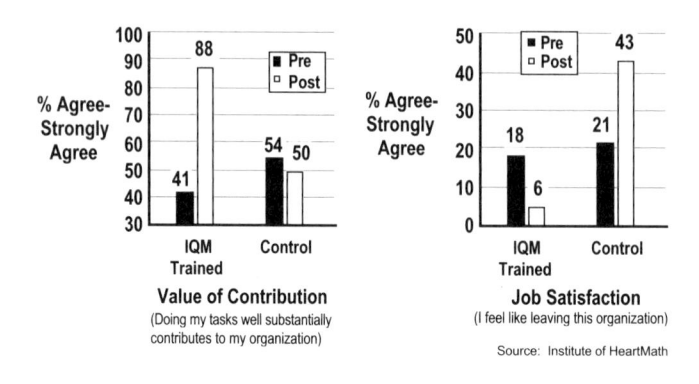

Value of Contribution
(Doing my tasks well substantially contributes to my organization)

% Agree-Strongly Agree — IQM Trained: Pre 41, Post 88; Control: Pre 54, Post 50

Job Satisfaction
(I feel like leaving this organization)

% Agree-Strongly Agree — IQM Trained: Pre 18, Post 6; Control: Pre 21, Post 43

Source: Institute of HeartMath

Job Satisfaction, as measured by the statement, "I feel like leaving this organization" improved among the trained group, but saw more than a 100% increase among those who were not trained. This has important implications for reducing turnover, recruitment costs, and replacement training costs.

Figure 42.
Improved Attitudes: Positive Outlook, Burnout

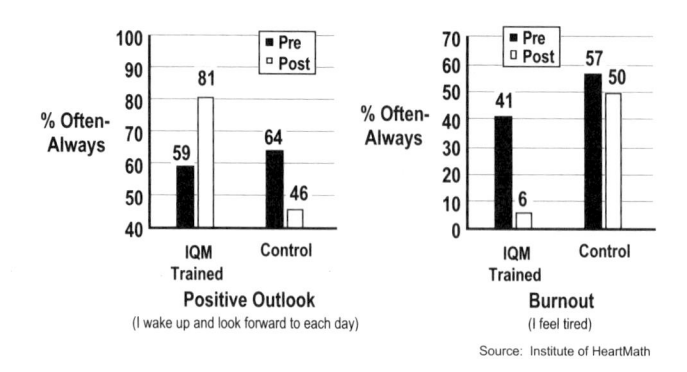

Positive Outlook
(I wake up and look forward to each day)

% Often-Always — IQM Trained: Pre 59, Post 81; Control: Pre 64, Post 46

Burnout
(I feel tired)

% Often-Always — IQM Trained: Pre 41, Post 6; Control: Pre 57, Post 50

Source: Institute of HeartMath

The trained group improved in Positive Outlook ("I wake up and look forward to each day") while the control group declined. Feelings of Burnout ("I feel tired") declined substantially among the trained group while the control group experienced almost no change. Feeling burned out is one of the factors that cause people to seek relief through prescription medications, a major health care cost concern of companies.

Figure 43.
Improved Performance: Quality of Work, Communication

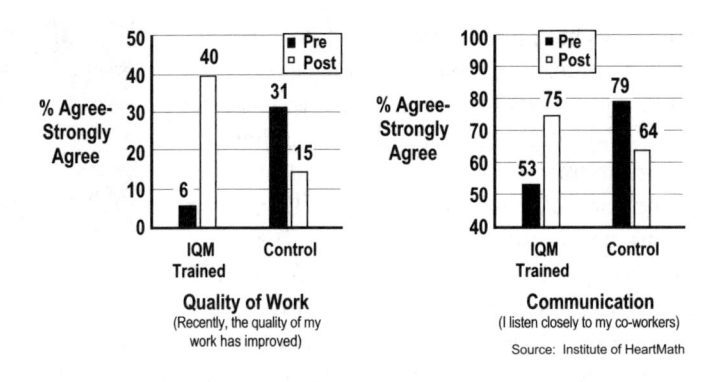

Quality of Work
(Recently, the quality of my work has improved)

- IQM Trained: Pre 6, Post 40
- Control: Pre 31, Post 15

Communication
(I listen closely to my co-workers)

- IQM Trained: Pre 53, Post 75
- Control: Pre 79, Post 64

Source: Institute of HeartMath

The trained group showed dramatic improvement in Quality of Work, from 6% to 40%, while the control group took a nosedive from 31% to 15%. Quality-related problems are a major cost factor that detracts from the company's bottom line. Similar results were experienced in Communication, with the trained group improving from 53% to 75%, while the control group slid from 79% to 64%.

Figure 44.
Improved Performance: Emotional Management, Physical Symptoms

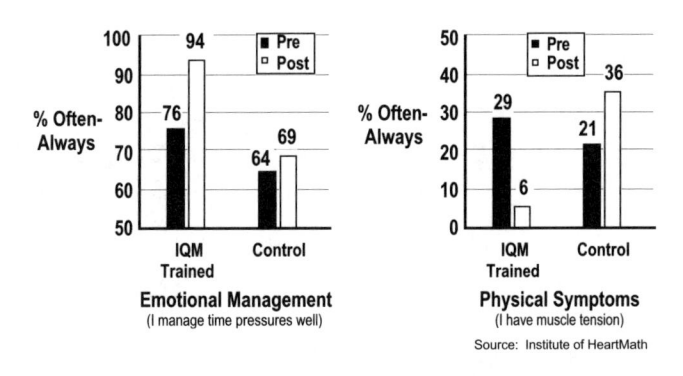

Emotional Management
(I manage time pressures well)

- IQM Trained: Pre 76, Post 94
- Control: Pre 64, Post 69

Physical Symptoms
(I have muscle tension)

- IQM Trained: Pre 29, Post 6
- Control: Pre 21, Post 36

Source: Institute of HeartMath

The trained group showed a 24% improvement, from 76% to 94%, in managing time pressure well, while the control group had a minor change. Physical health among the trained group also improved as the Physical Symptoms of stress ("I have muscle tension") declined from 29% to only 6%. The control group was not as fortunate; their tension rose from 21% to 36%, a 71% increase. Tension and other symptoms of stress are major factors causing health care costs to increase.

ABOUT THE AUTHOR

Byron Stock has taught applied Emotional Intelligence skill-building techniques to people in business, government and non-profits for 12 years. He pioneered a model for Emotional Intelligence skill-building that combines classroom training with personalized coaching, ensuring each person develops sustainable skills relevant to his or her work and personal life. He has delivered over 50 skill-building workshops and over 200 interactive presentations on the subject. Byron calls himself a "recovering engineer." He has 25 years of experience in human performance improvement and leadership development. He has held positions in Manufacturing Engineering, Design Engineering, Research and Engineering, Human Resources, Corporate Education, and Management and Leadership Development in Fortune 500 corporations.

He holds a B.S. in Industrial Engineering from Purdue University and an MBA from Xavier University. He is the President of Byron Stock & Associates LLC, a firm specializing in applied Emotional Intelligence skill-building training and coaching. Byron has been an Independent Certified Trainer with the Institute of HeartMath since 1995

ACKNOWLEDGEMENTS

If you're very lucky in life, you get to have a friend and colleague like Jane Shuman Sharratt. She convinced me to attend a training program where I learned, for the first time, about emotions. She created an approach that integrated personal goal-setting, training, and follow-up coaching which has helped make our Emotional Intelligence developmental programs so beneficial for our clients. I can't thank you enough for helping put me on the path I was meant to travel. Thank You!

April Frank would give you anything she had to help you. That's what she has done for me. I've had the pleasure of sharing ideas with April on almost a weekly basis for eleven years, not only about our work, but also about our lives. She cuts through the fog for me and enables me to see clearly. Thank you for giving me so much.

Thank you Jane and April, for speaking the truth in your suggestions on the first rough draft of the book. Your probing questions and observations made me reach deep inside and pull out a much better version of the book. A whack upside my head, from people who love me, is one of the best ways to get my attention. You've made this book much better.

To Esther Hopper, my editor, not only for the many improvements she suggested, but also for her enthusiasm for this subject and this book. She helped me hold my focus on both the purpose of the book and on my intended readers.

Thank you to LD Metcalfe, who not only read the entire rough draft, but also made extensive comments and recommendations. Your written and verbal support for the book convinced me that business people would read and benefit from it.

Thanks to Sherri Ingle for being an inspiration to me. Her resilience and energy is a model for me every day.

Bonnie Moore has brought me a heart and spirit-focused way of looking at the work I do. Listening to her always brings me back to center, the center I have within that is my true guide. When I listen to it, I always make the right decision. Thank you, Bonnie.

For sharing your experience and passion in writing a book about Emotional Intelligence, thank you, Pieter van Jaarsveld.

174 ACKNOWLEDGEMENTS

I am grateful to Cammie Hernandez, who tracked and recorded the thousands of inputs from first draft readers. How fortunate I am to have someone who makes details easy and funny.

I am deeply grateful to those who read the entire first rough (and I do mean rough) draft and made extensive comments and recommendations. Thank you Bob Crowley, Karla DonnellBragg, George Galante, Nancy Myers, Mary Nisbet, Mary Ellen Padin, Joanne Reid, Beth Smith Pfeil, Marcia Southall, Gayle Cutler, Doug Ingle, Jerry Sorenson, and others mentioned here separately.

I am deeply grateful to the friends, colleagues, business associates, and clients who reviewed the first rough draft of the book offering their evaluation of the stories and client comments. I know it was tedious work and I appreciate your persistence and care. Thank you, John Amrhein, Susan Barela, Edward Barlow Jr., Ray Bennett, Jim Bibbings, Janet Bieschke, Stephen Blair, Mabel Casey, Trish Chambers, Patrick Chantelois, Debbie and Gus Damaske, Jeff Davis, Chad DeKing, Mike Eads, Jeff Fierstein, Kent Gawart, Steve Goldberg, Gaylon Hayes, Faye Hobbs, Tom Howell, Danny Jackson, Ray Kennedy, Karen Kramer, Bill Langbehn, Nick Little, Leslie McCain, Linda Milanowski, Marg Mojzak, Nancy Myers, Paul Nickason, Brian Nisbet, Joe Nowicki, Cathy Rafferty, Chris Schumacher, Jerry Scott, Mark Shurman, Sam Somers, Michael Tilbrooke, Alma Triplett, Sheila Warfield, Judy Winiarz, and Laura Vriesman.

Thank you to all of the participants in our workshops for all I have learned from you and all you have helped me become. You have no idea how much joy you gave me when I listened to you tell me how you were improving your lives.

To those of you who were brave and persistent enough to convince your leaders to offer our program in your organization, I thank you. You are the pathfinders who have opened the door for people in your organizations to improve their lives. You have created a lasting legacy in many people's lives.

To those who receive our weekly emails and send us notes telling us your own story, all of our staff thank you.

When I see my friend Jim Bartley, I smile inside. He reminds me of the power the techniques have to change people's lives. Thanks big guy.

To Michael Kirton, my email friend in Australia, I extend my appreciation for his ongoing words of encouragement and confidence.

ACKNOWLEDGEMENTS

Thank you is an inadequate sentiment when it comes to the people at HeartMath LLC, and the Institute of HeartMath. I especially thank:
- Doc Childre whose insight, vision, persistence, and energy created the Institute and the techniques that have helped so many people.
- Bruce Cryer, for your counsel and support of my work and ideas.
- Howard Martin, the teacher who showed me the importance of being a model of this work.
- Gaby Boehmer and Elysia Cryer for there patience in verifying the Institute of HeartMath intellectual property presented in this book.
- Kim Allen, expert trainer and facilitator, who always shared ideas of how to make what I taught more grounded and real.
- All of the research staff at the Institute, for the groundbreaking work you do and the patience you exhibit in getting it published.

Thank you, Blair, for your encouragement and for politely keeping me on task. Luke, you provided insight and understanding beyond your years. Who could ask for better sons?

Sara, your ideas on how to reorganize the book made it so much better. Not only did you improve it, you enabled me to see how I could improve it further. How fortunate I am to have you for a daughter.

To Kiersten and John, I'm so thankful you are in our lives. To my grandchildren, Abby, Kaden, Ella, Lily, and Wren, you make Grandpa happy every time I'm with you or even think about you! Thank you for the joy of your love.

If I missed anyone, please know I thank you in my heart.

Finally, I thank my loving and patient wife, Nancy. She has supported me in everything I've ever wanted to do, and has raised our children to be wonderful adults. Her quiet persistence through adversity has shown me anything is possible. I love you!

REFERENCES

Boyatzis, Richard, Michelle Burckle, Hay Acquisition I Inc., 2000.
Buckingham, Marcus. "Idea Fest" *Fast Company Magazine* January 2003: 95 – 107.
Eysenck, H.J. "Personality, Stress and Cancer: Prediction and Prophylaxis." *British Journal of Medical Psychology,* 1988: *61,* 57-75.
Goleman, Daniel. *Emotional Intelligence: Why it can matter more than IQ.* New York: Bantam Books, 1995.
Goleman, Daniel. "What Makes a Leader?" *Harvard Business Review*, Nov/Dec 1998: 93-102.
Goleman, Daniel, Richard Boyatzis, Annie McKee. *Primal Leadership: Realizing the Power of Emotional Intelligence.* Boston: Harvard Business School Press, 2002.
Hafen, B., K. Frandsen, et al. *The Health Effects of Attitudes, Emotions and Relationships.* Provo, EMS Associates, 1992.
Houghton Mifflin. The *American Heritage Dictionary,* 1985.
Institute of HeartMath, *Inner Quality Management.* 1998.
Institute of HeartMath, *Research Overview.* HeartMath Research Center, 1997.
Kouzes, J. M. and Posner, Barry Z. "The Best Learning Practices of the Best Leaders," *The Leader's Almanac, (*Summer 2005) Adapted from the *Leadership Practices Inventory: Leadership Development Planner, 2003 Edition* by James M. Kouzes and Barry Z. Posner San Francisco: Jossey-Bass/Pfeiffer, 2003.
Loehr, James E. *Stress for Success: The Proven Program for Transforming Stress into Positive Energy at Work.* New York, Crown Business, 1997.
McCraty, R., B. Barrios-Choplin, D. Rozman, M. Atkinson, and A. D. Watkins. "The Impact of a New Emotional Self-Management Program on Stress, Emotions, Heart Rate Variability, DHEA and Cortisol." *Integrative Physiological and Behavioral Science* 33.2(1998): 151-70.
Shellenbarger, Sue. "Companies Are Finding It Really Pays To Be Nice To Employees," *Wall Street Journal,* 22 July 1998: B1.

ADDITIONAL BOOKS ON EMOTIONAL INTELLIGENCE

Anthony, Mitch. Selling With Emotional Intelligence; 5 Skills for Building Stronger Client Relationships. Chicago: Dearborn Trade Publishing, 2003.

Bradberry, Travis, and Jean Greaves. The Emotional Intelligence Quickbook; Everything You Need To Know To Put Your EQ To Work. New York: Simon & Schuster, 2005.

Caruso, David R., and Peter Salovey. The Emotionally Intelligent Manager; How to Develop and Use the Four Key Emotional Skills of Leadership. San Francisco: Jossey-Bass, 2004.

Cherniss, Cary, and Daniel Goleman. The Emotionally Intelligent Workplace; How to Select for, Measure, and Improve Emotional Intelligence in Individuals, Groups, and Organizations. San Francisco: Jossey-Bass, 2001.

Cooper, Robert K., and Ayman Sawaf. Executive EQ; Emotional Intelligence in Leadership & Organizations. New York: Grosset/Putnam, 1996.

Goleman, Daniel. Working With Emotional Intelligence. New York: Bantum Books, 1998.

Goleman, Daniel, Richard Boyatzis, Annie McKee. Primal Leadership; Realizing the Power of Emotional Intelligence. Boston: Harvard Business School Publishing, 2002.

Lynn, Adele B. B. The Emotional Intelligence Activity Book; 50 Activities for Promoting EQ at Work. New York: AMACOM, Division of American Management Association, 2001.

Rybak, David. Putting Emotional Intelligence To Work; Successful Leadership is More Than IQ. Oxford, UK: Butterworth Heinemann, 1998.

Salovey, Peter, and David Sluyter, EDS. Emotional Development & Emotional Intelligence; Educational Implications. New York: Basic Books/Harper Collins, 1997.

Weisinger, Ph.D., Hendrie. Emotional Intelligence at Work. San Francisco: Jossey-Bass, 1998.

BOOKS FROM HEARTMATH

Childre, Doc, and Bruce C. Wilson, M.D. *The HeartMath Approach to Managing Hypertension*. Oakland: New Harbinger Publications, 2007.

Childre, Doc, and Bruce Cryer. *From Chaos to Coherence*. Boulder Creek: HeartMath, 2000.

Childre, Doc, and Deborah Rozman, Ph.D. *Transforming Anger*. Oakland: New Harbinger Publications, 2003.

Childre, Doc, and Deborah Rozman, Ph.D. *Transforming Stress*. Oakland: New Harbinger Publications, 2005.

Childre, Doc, and Deborah Rozman, Ph.D. *Transforming Anxiety*. Oakland: New Harbinger Publications, 2006.

Childre, Doc, and Howard Martin. *The HeartMath Solution*. San Francisco: HarperSanFrancisco, 2000.

INDEX

A

Acknowledgements, 173
Action Planning, 56
Activate, 76, 79
   positive emotions, 14, 76
Amygdala, 31
ANS. *See* Autonomic Nervous System
Anxiety disorder, 33
Appreciation
   affects heart rhythms, 39
   and cortical facilitation, 39
   and entrainment, 41
   and Freeze-Frame, 76
   benefits of, 103
   clients' comments about, 141
   coaching/troubleshooting, 101
   debrief, 99
   effective, 95
   for consistent performance, 94
   for exceptional performance, 94
   for improved performance, 94
   impact of, 95
   in Heart Lock-In, 105
   ineffective, 95
   practicing, 99
   receiving, 98
   shorthand steps, 99
   steps of, 97
   stickers for, 101
   technique, 63, 92
   to create coherence, 103
   unusual reactions to, 100
   use in Intuitive Listening, 119
   when to express, 92
   why demonstrate, 93
Arrhythmia
   heart, 4, 33
Ask
   Step 4 of Freeze-Frame, 76
Asthma, 6, 33
Attitude
   and burnout, 170
   and job satisfaction, 170
   and Personal Goals, 149
   and positive outlook, 170
   and value of contribution, 170
   impacts revenue, 20
Author, 172
Autonomic Nervous System, 32
   "dis-ease" and, 33
   and diseases, 6
   and emotional memory, 32
   and Heart Lock-In, 107
   and negative emotions, 31
   Parasympathetic Pathway, 36
   Sympathetic Pathway, 36
Axon, 42

B

Balance
   and Autonomic Nervous System, 33
   and Personal Goals, 49, 147, 152
   work/life, 4, 13
Biological Oscillators
   and entrainment, 40
   defined, 40
Boyatsis, Richard, 19
Brain
   cell connectivity, 43
   emotional, 30
   first, 29
   function, 31
   impact of appreciation on, 103
   in the heart, 38
   Limbic, 30
   mid-level, 29
   Neocortex, 30
   neural circuits, 36
   positive emotions impact, 37
   Reptilian, 29
   second, 29
   thinking, 30
   third, 30
   three, 29
Brain waves
   frequency distribution of, 41
Brake pedal. *See* Parasympathetic Pathway
British Journal of Medical Psychology, 21
Buckingham, Marcus, 19, 25

C

Change
- and Freeze-Frame, 75
- and Personal Goals, 49, 151
- biochemical, 35
- due to Heart Lock-In, 110
- in heart rhythm, 105
- in perception, 36
- multiple, 24
- old patterns, 134
- physiological, 36
- real, 24

Change effectiveness, 23
Childre, Doc, v, 175, 178
Chronic fatigue, 6, 33
Coaching, 8
- for Appreciation, 101
- for Freeze-Frame, 89
- for Heart Lock-In, 111
- for Intuitive Listening, 125
- for What Am I Feeling Right Now?, 71
- Note Sheet, 56
- peer, 48, 56

Coherence, 40
- and biological systems, 103
- inner, 41

Coherent Perspective, 79, 80, 82
Comments
- about Personal Goals, 145
- about techniques, 139

Conflict, 4, 13, 48
- reduction, 157
- resolve/manage, 49

Cortical facilitation, 37, 39
Cortical inhibition, 37
Cortisol, 108, 109
Creativity, 49
Culture, 4, 19
Customer service, 25, 101
- and emotion, 25

D

Data, 162
- creative professionals, 162
- directors, 162
- executives. *See*
- high potentials, 162
- hypertension study, 162
- Information Technology team, 162
- leaders, 162
- managers, 162
- post, 168
- post-training, 167
- pre, 168
- pre-training, 167
- vice-presidents, 162

Death, 33
- and emotional stress, 21

Decision Guide, 1
Decision-making, 3, 5, 67
- and Personal Goals, 49, 147
- and positive emotion, 37
- and self-confidence, 49
- and self-leadership, 17
- moment-to-moment, 5
- poor, 4, 13

Dendrite, 42
Depression, 4, 6, 33, 103
DHEA
- decreased, 109
- fountain of youth hormone, 108
- increased, 109

Disease, 6
- cardiovascular, 21

Dis-ease, 33, 40
Dizziness, 33
Doing, 7
Dysrhythmia
- in ANS, 6

E

Electromagnetic
- energy, 40
- energy from the heart, 105
- field, 39

Email
- free, 8
- reminder, 8
- weekly, 8

Emotion
- affects heart rhythm, 36
- affects your abilities, 13
- and "dis-ease", 33
- and ANS imbalance, 33
- and best ideas, 39
- and biochemical change, 35
- and change, 23
- and cortisol, 108
- and customer service, 25
- and DHEA, 108
- and Emotional Intelligence, 11
- and Freeze-Frame, 75

and health, 21
and Heart Lock-In, 104
and hormones, 108
and Intuitive Listening, 116
and leadership, 18
and learning, 42
and music, 105
and perception, 35, 70
and performance, 21
and physical coordination, 31
and stress, 3, 4, 20
and the Appreciation technique, 99
appreciation, 39
as energy, 66
choosing, 14
defined, 65
economic value of, 19
hiding, 14
identifying, 66
impact on biological systems, 40
impact on immune system, 34
impacts brain function, 37
mismanaged, 4
negative, 5, 31, 66
physiological effects, 35
positive, 5, 65, 71
recognizing, 69
transforming, 14
triggers of negative, 69
when to pay attention to, 67
Emotional
  benefits, 48
  brain, 30, 31
  competencies, 12
  connection, 25
  hijacking, 32
  hormonal axis, 108
  Intelligence defined, 3
  memory, 32
  reactiveness, 49
  roller coaster, 23
  Self-awareness, 12, 13, 63
  Self-Awareness Pocket Card, 66
  Self-Awareness technique, 48, 68
  Self-management, 22
  Self-motivation, 12, 14
  Self-Motivation technique, 74
  Self-regulation, 12, 14
  Self-Regulation technique, 74
  skills, 63
  stress, 21
  triggers, 23
  vocabulary, 63, 66
Emotional Intelligence
  and decision-making, 3
  and leadership, 18
  benefits, 5
  competencies, 12
  development program, 9
  purpose, 11
  purpose of, 3
  the science of, 29
  what is, 11
Empathy, 14
  and Personal Goals, 150
  defined, 14
  Emotional Intelligence competencies, 12
Energy, 42
  and Appreciation technique, 94
  and Heart Lock-In, 103
  and Neutral, 89
  and Personal Goals, 146
  electromagnetic, 40
  emanates from the heart, 105
  emotion is, 65
  heart, 45
  managing, 72
  negative, 66
  positive, 65
  sending, 105
  wasted, 117
Entrainment, 40
  head/heart, 40

F

Feelings, 5
  and Freeze-Frame, 76
  and Heart Lock-In, 105
  and Intuitive Listening, 119
  and thoughts, 82
  negative, 5
  of burnout, 170
  positive, 5, 76
Fibromyalgia, 33
Fight, 30, 31, 108
First Break All the Rules, 19
Flight, 30, 31, 108
Free resources, 8
Freeze-Frame
  After situatioins, 86
  and Appreciation, 97
  and biological coherence, 41
  and Emotional Self-Regulation, 74
  and Intuitive Listening, 119
  and Personal Goals, 55, 145

Before situations, 86
clients' comments, 140
coaching for, 89
defined, 75
During situations, 86
eyes-open, 88
in an emergency, 133
other uses for, 84
practice, 79, 88
Practice Sheet, 79
shorthand steps, 79
steps of, 76
stickers, 88
technique, 75
when to use, 74, 85
Frequency distribution
of brain waves, 40
of heart beats, 40

G

Gas pedal. *See* Sympathetic Pathway
Goal and Situation Note Sheet, 50
Goleman, Daniel, 18, 19

H

Headache
and Personal Goals, 49, 146
migraine, 4, 103
Health, 6, 21
and Heart Lock-In, 103
immune system, 35
Heart
and brain "in sync", 40, 41
and Freeze-Frame, 76
and Heart Lock-In, 104
and Intuitive Listening, 119
and Personal Goals, 146
ANS connection, 32
arrhythmia, 4, 33
attack, 134
beat, 38
brain in the, 38
communicates with the brain, 38
during first hour of sleep, 111
in fetus, 38
influences the brain, 38
pacemaker cells, 40
produces electromagnetic field, 39
resting rate, 36
rhythms, 36, 39
the dominant oscillator, 40

to brain, 38
Heart Rate Variability, 36
HeartMath. *See* Institute of HeartMath
Heart-To-Brain Communication, 38
HPA. *See* Hypothalamus/ Pituitary/ Adrenal
HRV. *See* Heart Rate Variability
Hypertension, 6, 33
study, 162
Hypoglycemia, 6, 33
Hypothalamus/ Pituitary/ Adrenal axis, 108

I

IgA. *See* Immunoglobulin A
Immune system, 33, 35
Immunoglobulin A, 33
In sync
biological oscillators, 40
Influence others
and Personal Goals, 49
Information Technology, 9, 132, 162, 165
Institute of HeartMath, v, 36, 103, 134, 175
Interpersonal Competencies, 14
Interpersonal skills. *See* Interpersonal Competencies
Intrapersonal Competencies, 13
Intrapersonal skills. *See* Intrapersonal Competencies
Intuitive Listening
and Empathy, 114
and Personal Goals, 55, 148
Chinese character for, 118
clients' comments, 143
coaching, 125
eliminates resistance, 129
influencing others, 157
practice, 122
purpose, 116
shorthand version, 120
steps, 119
stickers, 125
technique, 114
use of, 125
when to use, 114, 120
Irritable Bowel Syndrome, 33

K

Knowing, 7
Koznes, James, 19

L

Leadership
  and emotions, 18
  practices, 19
  self, 17
Limbic System, 31
Listening. *See* Intuitive Listening
Loehr, James, 25

M

Map, 1
  SMART Emotions, 2, 7
McKee, Annie, 19
Mental clarity
  and Appreciation, 92
  and Freeze-Frame, 84
  and Personal Goals, 49, 147
  lack of, 4
Mitral valve prolapse, 33
Morale
  and Personal Goals, 49, 158
Motivation. *See* Emotional Self-Motivation
  personal, 47
Music
  "Heart Zones" CD, 106, 143
  and Heart Lock-In, 105
  favorite, 131

N

Neocortex, 30
Nervous system. *See* Autonomic Nervous System
Neural circuitry
  development of new, 88
Neural circuits, 36
Neuron, 42
  defined, 38
Neutral, 88
  and Personal Goals, 148
  benefits, 89

P

Pacemaker cells, 40
Panic disorder, 33
Parasympathetic Pathway. *See* Autonomic Nervous System
Peer Coaching, 56
  Note Sheet, 56

Perception Cycle, 35
Performance
  and Appreciation, 93, 97
  and Heart Lock-In, 108
  and Personal Goals, 146
  consistent, 94
  exceptional, 94
  how change impacts, 24
  how emotions impact, 20
  improved, 94
  increase, 5
  ingredients of excellent, 18
  managing emotions improves, 21
  physical, 31
  unsatisfactory, 4
Personal Goals
  and Situation Note Sheet, 50
  and Techniques Matrix, 55
  clients' comments, 47, 145
  improvements in, 26, 163, 165
  listing of, 48
  Peer Coaching on, 56
  selecting, 48
  what you want to improve, 3
Personal Goals/Techniques Matrix, 7. *See*
Personal motivation, 47
  and Personal Goals, 149
  sources of, 47
Posner, Barry, 19
Premenstrual syndrome, 33
Primal Leadership, 19
Productivity
  and Personal Goals, 49, 148
  impact of Apprecition on, 95

Q

Quick Information, 1
  Decision Guide, 1
  free resources, 8
  SMART Emotions is unique, 7
  SMART Emotions Map, 2

R

Relationships, 6
  and Personal Goals, 49, 154, 155
  impact of Appreciation on, 95
  nurturing, 12, 15
Remembering
  stickers, 8
  will make you successful, 47
Results

additional, 28
clients' comments, 139, 145
data, 162
illustrative stories, 129
of eight-month follow-up, 166
sample, 26
Revenue, 20

S

Science
  of Emotional Intelligence, 29
Sears, Roebuck and Company, 20
Self-confidence
  and Personal Goals, 49, 149
Self-leadership, 17
Shorthand version
  of Appreciation, 99
  of Freeze-Frame, 79
  of Heart Lock-In, 105
  of Intuitive Listening, 120
  of WAIFRN, 68
Situations
  After, 86
  Before, 86
  During, 86
  future, 69
  past, 68
  Personal Goals, 50
  real business, 7
  that trigger negative emotions, 63
  that trigger your emotions, 69
  to use Appreciation, 92
  to use Freeze-Frame, 74
  to use Heart Lock-In, 106
  to use Intuitive Listening, 114
  to use WAIFRN, 64
  your specific, 7
Sleep
  disorders, 33
  first hour of, 111
Sleeplessness, 4
  and Personal Goals, 49
  decreased, 146
  elimination of, 6
  reduction of, 103
Social-awareness, 69
Stickers
  free reminder, 8
Stories
  illustrative, 129
Stress, 20
  an internal reaction, 21
  and Freeze-Frame, 76
  and Personal Goals, 49, 146
  bad, 21
  curve, 22
  defined, 3
  emotional, 21
  eustress, 21
  good, 21
  hormone, 35, 108
  impact of, 4
  job, 79
  managing, 165
  personal, 83
  physical symptoms of, 171
  reduced symptoms of, 167
Stress for Success, 25
Support
  coaching, 71, 89, 101, 111, 125
  reminder stickers, 8
  weekly email, 8
Sympathetic Pathway. *See* Autonomic Nervous System

T

Teamwork
  and Personal Goals, 49, 159
  impact of Appreciation on, 101
  lack of, 4
Techniques
  and Personal Goals Matrix, 55
  Appreciation, 92
  build skills, 63
  clients' comments about, 139
  five simple, 63
  Freeze-Frame, 75
  Heart Lock-In, 103
  Intuitive Listening, 114
  primary, 55
  proven, vi, 5
  remembering, 47
  secondary, 55
  What Am I Feeling Right Now?, 64
The Leadership Challenge, 19
Threats
  physical, 23
  symbolic (psychological), 23
Triggers
  and the Perception Cycle, 36
  emotional, 23
  identify your own, 70
  of negative emotions, 69
  sample, 69

universal, 23
your, 50, 69

U

Unique
   about this book, 7

V

Vagus nerve, 38
Value
   and Appreciation, 99
   economic, 19
   of contribution, 170

W

WAIFRN. *See* What Am I Feeling Right Now?
What Am I Feeling Right Now?, 63
   clients' comments, 139
   coaching, 71
   practice, 69
   technique, 63, 68
   use, 71
   when to use, 64
What Makes a Leader?, 18
Worry
   and Personal Goals, 49, 146

LEADER'S GUIDE FOR SMART EMOTIONS

For Whom is This Leader's Guide Intended?
The Leader's Guide is for anyone who manages people at any level in any organization. Your title may be Team Leader, Supervisor, Manager, Director, Vice President, President, COO, or CEO. Titles don't matter — what does matter is…
- You sincerely care about your people.
- You want to help your people and yourself learn skills to deal with the stress and pressure of work.
- You see the value in developing these skills together.
- You are personally committed to applying what you learn and helping your people do the same.

Overview of the Process
The **SMART EMOTIONS Leader's Guide** is designed to assist you in leading discussions based on material in the **SMART EMOTIONS** book. Each staff member reads part of the **SMART EMOTIONS** book, answers the Focus Questions for that section, completes the required practices, and uses the techniques as recommended at work and at home. Meet with your people for 30 minutes at the beginning of your regularly scheduled staff meeting to discuss the Focus Questions, any other questions people have about what they have read, and discuss how using the techniques will positively impact individuals, the team, and overall performance.

Structure of the Leader's Guide
Each section of the guide is organized with checkboxes and straightforward "what to dos." Space for your personal notes and examples is provided so that you can be prepared to share your experiences with your team concerning your thoughts about the information and techniques in **SMART EMOTIONS**. Space is also provided for note taking as members of your staff raise questions or make points about how the material applies to work problems and difficulties.

How This Guide Will Help You Lead Sessions
This guide prepares you to be in control and successful in leading discussions around the various topics, concepts, and techniques presented in **SMART EMOTIONS**. It provides what you need to coach your entire team as you and they develop critically important Emotional Intelligence skills.

To order the **SMART EMOTIONS Leader's Guide** *or for more information call 269-429-1833, email info@ByronStock.com, or visit our website at www.ByronStock.com.*

TRAINING PROGRAMS, SEMINARS, AND WORKSHOPS

Byron Stock & Associates provides applied Emotional Intelligence skill-building programs for organizations and individuals. These highly effective programs have been shown to dramatically improve performance and relationships. Skill-building training is available through on-site programs for organizations and sponsored public workshops, seminars, and conference presentations.

For information on training programs, coaching programs, and products call 269-429-1833, or visit our website at www.ByronStock.com.